CW00972001

W

The information c

book is to be used at your own risk.

The writer of this publication is not

responsible for any paranoia,

injuries or death stemming from the

contents of this book. Some of the

ideas or homemade projects can

cause injury and should be used

with caution and adult supervision.

This book has been written for and
dedicated to my family and friends.

I want this book to help people in their
time of need and to help them feel better
about any situation they may be in with
their own families in troubled times.

When an emergency is upon you the time for
preparation has passed.

The prudent see danger and take refuge, but the
simple keep going and suffer for it. Proverbs 27:12

To my fellow Christians:

God be with you and bless you in troubled times.

Table of Contents

The Urban Survivalist Handbook

The goal of the urban survivalist is not to fight the government or to be an extremist. The goal of the urban survivalist is to weather any unforeseen event. These events may include anything from a natural disaster to civil unrest due to an economic collapse. The way I describe an urban survivalist is a person who is prepared and can overcome any crisis by using pre existing storage, knowledge and common sense.

People may look at the urban survivalist like a paranoid person. However, think about this! The people who fared the best during Hurricane Katrina were survivalists. They already had food stored up when others went hungry. The urban survivalist had potable water while others became dehydrated. The urban survivalist had power or other means to cook and endure the situation.

The urban survivalist also had the means to protect themselves from looters and gang members that ran amuck before order was restored. In some areas it took FEMA seven days to get to stranded Americans. Ask yourself can you survive for seven days without water, power, septic, gas, A/C or a heater? The urban survivalist is ready and can weather any situation. In a nut shell the urban survivalist is a grown-up boy scout.

In 2007 Italy was being strangled by a trucker and transportation strike, mostly because of high gas prices but there were other issues as well. However the country began to break down only after three days. Grocery stores shelves began to run bare and gas stations closed because they had ran dry. It amazed me that people were going hungry by the third day. The stores that still had product, doubled and tripled the prices. You always have to remember the rule of supply vs. demand. If it is in demand it's going to be expensive if there is minimal demand the price goes down. This could easily happen here in America.

If you don't think that anything has happened already that would constitute preparing then think about this. On Thursday, August 14, 2003 an untrimmed tree and an overloaded power line left 55 million people without power and most of them were out of power for a 24 hour period. During the outage water pumps stopped and began limiting the amount of potable water available to citizens. Sewer treatment plants were unable to close certain flow gates causing contaminated water. Anyone who was able to get gasoline was being charged double for it.

Hospitals were running on diesel generators and by the end of the power outage they were running low on fuel and causing a whole set of problems. Everyone was on a boil your water advisory until 4 days after the power outage. This was all for a 24 hour blackout. This blackout lasted only 24 hours, now think what the ramifications would be if you were out of power for one week, two weeks or even one month. Once the power goes out several things start to happen. First water pressure begins to drop and sewage pumps come to a grinding halt. Frozen and refrigerated foods begin to spoil and communications break down.

Soon low level thugs begin looting and seizing the opportunity to conduct their crimes. This is why we need to prepare our lives and our homes to protect yourself and your family.

December 19th 2009 West Virginia received 20 inches of snow and knocked out power for 60,000 people leaving them in the cold. The Urban Survivalist will be prepared and would not have to go out in the brutal weather to get food, water, or things to heat or light the house. Take a moment and ask yourself if you were to get snowed in and find yourself without power, would you be prepared?

On December 21st, 2009 Valdez, Alaska had been in a severe storm dropping more than 4 inches of snow an hour. By the time the snow fall stopped the official measurement was 5 feet 8 inches deep of the white stuff. If the people of Valdez were not prepared and no help came, they would be dead.

With the bird flu and the new H1N1 (Swine flu) out breaks, people are afraid of going out into public. If a person was trying to stay away from others to avoid getting sick and wanted to stay indoors would they be prepared. Would they have the provisions and the knowledge to stay safe and healthy? If a pandemic were to break out it could bring a whole metropolis to its knees and if you are not prepared you will have to risk exposure to get supplies or food.

If you don't think that an outbreak will happen here in America then ask the residence of Milwaukee. In 1993 Milwaukee had a Cryptosporidium outbreak which got in to the drinking water due to the city's treatment plants inability to filter out the parasite. 54 people died and 403,000 people became ill within a two week period and virtually shut down the city.

According to the American Society of Civil Engineers America's power infrastructure needs a minimum of 1.2 trillion dollars to upgrade the grid to simply prevent a collapse. The power companies cannot foot this bill and the government has given a few billion to upgrade infrastructure from the bailout bill. This is placing a Band-Aid on a wound made by an out of control chainsaw. As the power grid become out of date, overloaded, and broken down we will experience brown outs, black outs and the possibility of long periods of powerless lifestyles.

According to the American Society of Civil Engineers our 2009 infrastructure report card is currently rated at a D overall. They also say that it will cost 2.2 trillion dollars to upgrade out failing grade of a D to a B.

They rate America's infrastructure as the following:

Bridges	C
Dams	D
Drinking water	D-
Levees	D-
Roads	D-
Wastewater	D-
Power Grid	D+
Schools	D
Solid Waste	C+
Transit	D
Inland Waterways	D-

These are all ticking time bombs and can devastate our way of life. If any one of these infrastructure systems fails and you are not prepared you may suffer inconveniences like no other. You can find the facts at www.asce.org

With the price of gasoline rising and the fight against fossil fuels, the prices or only going to increase causing an already volatile situation to worsen. Most of the major oil supplies of the world are not friends of the United States. We are facing more obstacles in the future than any other time in history. Granted here in the USA we get some of our oil from Canada and South America.

However South America has been slowing production due to a decrease in supply. We are dependent on oil and with OPEC running the industry we are susceptible to their manipulation of the market. If the price of oil begins to rise to levels that the normal person can no longer afford to fill the gas tank to make it to work the system will break and what will you do.

If the Middle East wanted to hurt the United States they have the weapon of economic mass destruction. We need to get off of our dependency for foreign energy to ensure our future. I may not have the answers to the troubles in the USA but I do know how to get through them.

Another thing that we need to think about is Hyperinflation. Hyperinflation is an inflationary cycle without the tendency towards equilibrium. Hyperinflation is a vicious cycle that can continue to increase the cost of all goods and services. As the hyperinflation cycle continues and prices sky rocket, hording and price gouging go into effect.

For example, let's say that a loaf of bread costs you $1.99 today and then you introduce hyperinflation. Now the same loaf of bread could cost $10.00 and a month later even $100.00. How does this happen you ask? Through the destabilization of our currency. With the bailouts and the Federal Reserve printing vast amounts of money without backing, the value of our dollar is now in a down turn.

Now think about this, add in the fact that other counties are holding vast amounts of our treasury bonds. China holds more than 700 billion dollars in treasury bonds. If China or any other country decides that they no longer want the bonds and cash all the bonds in our dollar could fall and the American people would go through times worst than the great depression ever saw. I just want you to understand that our fate may not be in our hands and if you prepare yourself, you and your family can get through any situation.

We are also facing the worse debt crisis in American history. The deficit is now 12 trillion dollars and rising. With a large debt America is at a cross roads. First America can default and go through one of the worst economic times in this country's history or America can try to tackle the debt by cutting spending and all government programs thus causing extremely hard economic times.

We are at a time in history when we face a harsh future. The United Nations estimates that the world population in 2050 will be 8.9 billion people. Most experts say that they are underestimating the population growth and with the current water usage and food production the globe can only sustain 9 billion people. With this information anyone can see that we are truly primed for a coming crisis.

As humans we believe we are masters of our universe. The truth is we are but a speck in this vast universe and the solar system has some surprises for us. Two things have hit the earth in the past and the same two things will hit earth again at some point in time. First we have no protection from the universe sending asteroids and meteors our way. Earth is hit thousands of times a day by meteors and it is only a matter of time before we get hit by one that causes devastation. Second our sun can be dangerous to our way of life. Starting in 2010 and going into 2013 NASA predicts the worst solar flare activity in history. A strong solar flare can have the same effect as an EMP thus ending our way of life with our power grid.

When I was growing up I was very lucky. I grew up on a small farm in southeastern New Mexico. As a rule farmers are survivalists. There were several family members living within a couple acres of us. It was like a small co op between all the family members we had cows, chickens, pigs, rabbits and a half acre garden. We were on well water and had propane for cooking and heat. This is an ideal situation. However as life happens and we grow older I now find myself in Phoenix AZ. with a wife and kids living in a nice stucco home in a sea of other homes that look the same.

I think back to the times of my childhood and remember my grandma canning and making jelly from the fruit trees. I realized that my grandparents had lived during the great depression and now have skills that need to be passed on to generation X before it is lost forever. As I started to further my education about self reliance I also watched as our country began to fall into a recession.

I have also thought about the millions of terrorist that hate America and will do just about anything to kill us. They did it once just remember the attacks on September 11th 2001. For those of us who lives on the border we see the violence spill over every day. Mexico has a depressed economy and a severe drug cartel problem which spills over the borders and American citizens sometimes pays the price. Canada and Mexico do not have some of the same Intel as our government and terrorist can come to these countries and make their way to ours.

This is yet another reason to prepare for unforeseen events or disasters. We think that we are safe and we have become complacent in everyday life. This is why we get blindsided and then begin asking what happened and how did this happen. Most of the time, we have no one to blame besides ourselves and our governments unwillingness to guard the borders adequately and take the necessary precautions to protect our nation.

We need to use our power of the right to vote as American citizens and vote in people who will safeguard our nation. Until that happens it is now up to you to take your own precautions and adequately guard your own home by becoming an urban survivalist.

Bad things have happened in the past such as terrorist, recessions, depressions, and economic collapses. There have been pandemics, epidemics and natural disasters. To see the future look to the past, for history always repeats itself. This is when I decided I will be prepared; I will be the urban survivalist.

1) The Basics

The first step to becoming an urban survivalist is to think about going camping. What do you need to sustain yourself and live in the woods for a week? If something happens where you live you may loss all of your utility's. Having no power and no running water is essentially camping. Your home is your tent or your camper and the food you have is it, unless you gather more. Lastly the water you have stored is all you will have unless you make or find more drinkable water.

You may think I will just go to the store and buy more. Now with everything being electronic most stores will not sell their product without electricity. Most stores will close and even if they do sell their product it will be on a cash basis only. Do you live off of a debit card or credit cards? Your cards will be useless. Do you keep a small amount of cash or gold coins in case of emergencies?

I know people that go to the grocery store almost every day to get dinner on their way home from work. These people will have an extremely hard time. If they have to rely on the government to provide for them, they are going to starve. Then we have to think about hyperinflation. It is supply and demand. If the supply is low and the demand is high the price goes way up. If you are like many other Americans living pay check to pay check and you are not prepared then you may not make it that is the simple truth.

If we enter into a prolonged depression or a national disaster that causes a national state of emergency millions of people will suffer and millions could die.

Now think about this. Worst case scenario, the country is in full civil unrest from an economic collapse and the government has implemented curfews and rationing on supplies. What are you going to do? How do you survive? What happens if the food rations stop? How do you feed your family?

Walk around your home and write down what you have and what you need. Think of bad situations and how you may get through them. Do you have food or water storage and how much? Do you fill confident that you can get through a severe event or natural disaster? By the end of this book hopefully you will have the answer to the previous question.

There are three essentials needed to sustain life. **Food, water** and **shelter**. Let us look at the first of the essentials food. Food comes in so many varieties and flavors along with multiple ways of packaging with different shelf dates. Then you need know how to rotate through your food and watch the expiration dates. The ends and outs of food storage will be covered in chapter 3 and should give you an insight to this new way of life.

The next essential is water. Water is vital to survival. Your body will begin to shut down after 3 days without water. Water is needed in winter and summer to keep up digestion and body functions. Water storage will be discussed in the next chapter.

Last on the essentials list is shelter. Shelter can be anything from a cardboard box to a mansion. Shelter is the means to keep a person alive and out of natures elements. Shelter is a basic need and a necessity. Preparing your shelter will be covered later in this book.

As you think about preparation and getting stocked up you may have to take it slow due to the cost of the products. I started preparing a few years ago and have found that as time goes on prices seem to be moving upward faster than I have ever seen before. I believe that this could be due to a couple of things. First the economic situation of our country and second the value of the falling dollar.

I have seen a substantial increase in food storage items and preparedness supplies. I believe that the prices are only going higher. If you are getting started I would have to say that I believe that your food storage may be the most important place to start. You probably already have a place to live or have a place to go. Water can be stored cheap and easily but your food storage can prove to be a challenge. Do you have enough money to get what you want and do you have a place to store it?

When storing water bottles or food it is a good idea to use the back of closets and under beds. If you can, use a full closet to store your food. The closet will stay cool and dark. Food and water storage can be prolonged by having both of these factors. I have utilized my entire closet in my office by building shelves and organizing it properly to hold most of my food storage and found it to work out very nicely.

Most people will have to start out small and obtain a little at a time. In the next chapters I will explain where and how to get short term and make long term food storage. I will tell you how to store water cheaply and how to improve your situation if anything were to happen causing you to go into survival mode.

With your food storage you must have a plan in place to be able to cook the food you have stored even if you don't have power or gas. You will also need to be able to get or make drinkable water to keep you hydrated and help you survive any situation. These are some of the things you will face in a disaster.

To become an urban survivalist you will need to give up a couple things. You will give up a little money, time, and storage space. However if you find yourself in a life or death situation the money you spent, the time that you provided and the storage space you used will save your life.

Let's get started.

2) Water procurement and water storage.

A grave natural disaster has occurred and you now find yourself without power or running water. What do you do at this point? Do you have a plan in place? Do you have supplies on hand? Let me introduce a new idea. Most people have a barbeque grill in the backyard. You are not sure how long this event will last so you want to ration your propane but you need to boil water. What do you do?

The urban survivalist can go to the living room and pull the lens out of the big screen TV. Are you confused, let me explain. The lens in a big screen TV is called a Fresnel lens. A Fresnel lens is a plastic lens that collects light and focuses it to the center causing a magnification. A typical Fresnel lens will yield around 1700-2000 degrees when used as a giant magnifying glass. With a Fresnel lens you can set up your lens and bounce the beam off of a mirror and onto the bottom of a frying pan. You can now cook or boil water with a totally renewable source of free energy.

The urban survivalist can now make any water drinkable. One thing you can do is start with a clean paint can or sealable metal container Next drill a ¼ inch hole in the top and place a brass fitting and a ¼ inch copper tubing into the hole and tighten the brass fitting. . Now you can use swamp water, salt water or dirty water and place it into the paint can or metal container.

The other end of the copper tubing is then placed into a clean container lower than the top of the metal container. You can place the can on a fire pit, stove or use the Fresnel lens. As the water boils the steam goes through the copper tube and condensates into distilled, pure water into the clean container. By using the Fresnel lens the urban survivalist can now save his propane for cloudy or rainy days.

If you do not have a Fresnel lens or want to supplement the Fresnel lens with a backup. A solar still is another great tool. A solar still is very simple to make and you probably have all the supplies in your home now. The urban survivalist can walk out to his back yard and dig a hole in a bowl shape. Next place a clean glass or cup in the very middle of the dirt bowl and then soak the ground with non potable water or even urine. Place a tube into the clean glass and run it to the edge of the dirt bowl. Now take plastic (black preferably) like a garbage bag and place over the dirt bowl and cover the edge of the bag with dirt all the way around. Now place a rock in the center of the bag right over the glass.

You have now made a solar still. The plastic will cause the ground to heat up and cause evaporation. The evaporated water will condensate on the plastic and run down the plastic to the middle and drip off into the glass. The water that ends up in the glass is pure and distilled. The tube that you placed into the glass is used to get the drinkable water out without disturbing the still. These little tricks could be the difference between staying healthy and becoming sick from dehydration or even death.

What do you do if you need to heat up water to bathe in or clean with? You can pull up the black plastic PVC irrigation line from your back yard or use a water hose and coil it into a large circle. Fill it with water and let it sit in direct sunlight. Within one hour the line well be almost too hot to touch and the water will be equally as hot.

There is another way to get water but it will not yield a great amount but in a pinch it could quench a thirst. This one is pretty simple. Get a plastic trash bag and then find a healthy tree branch with a lot of leaves. Place the transpiration bag over the branch. Place a rock at the bottom of the bag and tie the top of the bag around the branch. During the day the sun will heat up the bag and cause the water to evaporate out of the leaves. The water will then condensate on the bag and run down to the bottom of the bag where it can be harvested for drinking. However if the bag is left on the branch too long the branch will die and will not yield any more water.

When it comes to a point when you are trying to conserve or ration water you have to obtain water from every source possible. If it begins to rain, there are ways to collect the runoff that can yield a large amount of water. Typically during a mild rain one roof top can yield up to 600 gallons of water. There are several techniques that can be used. One is to use a tarp and attach one end to the underside of the roof. Then attach the other side to a pole making a J shape to catch the entire water running off from the roof.

It is advisable to let the water runoff of the roof for a few minutes to wash away any contaminates then begin collecting. If you do not have any bags, containers or barrels to catch the water then here is a little trick. Line the bed of a pickup truck with a tarp or plastic then pull the pickup under the gutter down spout or under the make shift tarp rain catch. Be sure to boil or distill all water collected to make sure you do not get sick form any contaminates that may come off of the roof such as bird droppings.

If an event happens and you need to store water quickly there is a trick to get a hundred plus gallons of water stored up fast. There are bags that you can purchase that in an event you simply place the bag into the bath tub and fill it up before water services stop. These bags can hold 50 to 65 gallons of potable water. If you fill one in each bath tube that is a quick 100 to 130 gallons of water that can help sustain life.

If you have the resources then you can make your own water purifier. I will tell you how to do it on a larger scale and if you need to you can scale it down. First take a clean plastic tubs or trash cans and drill several ¼ holes in the bottoms. Lay a filter, paper or cloth on the bottom of the tub and put a layer of sand in the tub about 3 to 4 inches thick. Now for the second layer I use small charcoal pieces 3 to 4 inches thick. If you have to, burn some wood and make your own charcoal do it. Now repeat sand and charcoal layering once more.

After you have the 2 layers of sand and 2 layers of charcoal stack the containers and place them above a collection barrel to gather the filtered water. The water out of the collection barrel now only has to be boiled and will be drinkable without any worry of contamination or bacteria. After boiling get a second pot and pour the water back and forth several times to aerate the water, this little technique will improve the taste.

A small version can be made quick and easy using a two litter bottle, cloth, sand, gravel and charcoal.

First you will need to prep the bottle. Using a razor blade cut the bottom off of the bottle. The bottom can be turned around and placed back into the bottom of the bottle to be used as a large debris filter and water catch.

Next drill a small hole into the bottom of each low spot of the bottom piece.

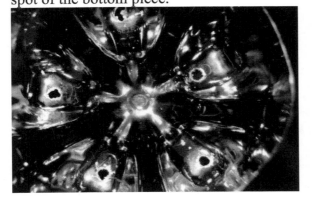

Now remove the cap from the top of the two litter bottle and drill 3 or 4 1/8th inch holes into the cap.

Next you will need some charcoal, sand and gravel. Sand and gravel can be found easily but as far as charcoal goes I suggest you make your own. I advise against using store bought charcoal due to the fact that chemicals are added to commercial charcoal to help with combustion.

Using a towel or old clean shirt and cut a 6 inch square, fold it up and push the wade of cotton into the neck of the bottle. Next cut several more 6 inch squares. Now place the piece of shirt or towel in the bottle and then gravel. Place another layer of cloth and add a layer of charcoal then another layer of cloth and put in a layer of sand. Lastly place a layer of pee gravel on top of the sand.

Dirty or contaminated water can be placed into the top of the filter. It will take about 1 hour for the water to get through the filter. Use a clean glass to catch the filtered water. It is always advisable to boil the filtered water as a precaution.

At some camping or outdoor stores you can find a product called a Life Straw. The Life Straw is about $25.00 and is basically a straw with a filer that can provide you with 300 gallons of drinking water. The taste of the water may be a little subpar however it will sustain life without getting you sick. All in all it is worth the money and can be easily carried anywhere.

There are cheaper versions as well. Aquamira sells an Emergency Water Filter System and cost around $7.00. However this straw will only filter about 20 gallons.

If you have a swimming pool then you have water storage. Most pools hold between 10,000 and 15,000 gallons. You need to boil, distill, filter or treat the water before drinking it but you will be better off than most people.

Another method of water procurement that I will be covering is going to take place in the morning time. First find a large grassy area and go there just before sunrise. Now take a sheet and begin dragging it over the grass to collect the dew. As your sheet becomes wet you can stop and wring out the sheet into a bucket. Depending on how big of an area you are dragging you can get up to a gallon of water a day. Once you are done then you can pour the water through a piece of cloth or a coffee filter to remove any debris and always boil the water before drinking it.

When it comes to collecting water you may only be able to get a little bit of water here and there. You will need to use all of your resources to get enough water to keep you and your family healthy. There are many ways to get water and I recommend you research the subject further for different methods that correspond to your area, IE desert, arctic, forest, or the plains.

If you have water stored up then you will be better off then the next guy but now you can use these techniques to help ration the water that you have. Several years ago I had just started storing water and my wife seemed annoyed by the whole thing. Then a short time later we were told not to drink the city water or boil it before using. Something happened to the city water system and it took about one week before the news came we could trust the city water system again. Now during this, it was nice to walk into the garage and get a pan of water and not worry if it is going to make me or my family sick.

There are several options of storing water and it depends on your storage space and amount you want. There is a variety of containers that you can use. The containers range from 55 gallon drums to 2 liter bottles. It is up to you which ones you use. The rule of thumb for water is to have at least 1 gallon of water per person per day in your household for at least one week. This is the bare minimum.

If you are filling up your containers and are using well water then you need to add 6 to8 drops of bleach per gallon to treat the water for storage. If you are on city water, the city has already treated the water for you and no further treatment is necessary. The water in your containers requires two things. First keep the container out of direct sunlight. Sunlight will cause algae to grow in your container and render the water undrinkable. Second the water needs to be changed once a year. Simply pour out the water and rinse the container out then refill it. I recommend writing the date on the container to keep track of the freshness of the water.

I have several different types of water storage. First I have several 55 gallon drums in my garage. Second I have multiple 5 and 6 gallon jugs stored in the back of the closets where they are out of the way and if I need to leave my home but want to take potable water with me I can.

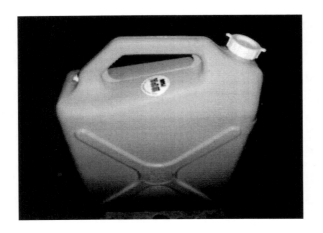

Third, once I finish a two litter bottle of soda I then wash out the bottle and fill it with water date it and store it. If space is limited and I have to leave my house two litter bottles are easy to carry and transport.

If you decide that you want to use 55 gallon drums for water storage there is one thing that you should remember. If storing the barrels on concrete you should place a couple 2X4's on the floor and place the barrels on the 2X4's. If the barrel is stored on the concrete the barrel will sweat and after a long period of time this process begins to eat away at the bottom of your barrel.

I would recommend against using milk jugs or water stored in these types of jugs. The sides are too weak and can puncture way to easy possibly causing water damage to your home. I have dropped a gallon jug of water on accident on the carpet and when it hit the floor it acted like a bomb and the jug split from the top to the bottom. I have also dropped a two litter bottle on the concrete and it only bounced and rolled around. However if this is all you have then store the water but store the jugs in a place where it will not damage anything if one were to leak or bust. Any water storage is better than no water storage.

It is a good idea to keep a bottle of bleach on hand if you need to treat water for drinking. As stated before you should add 6 to 8 drops of bleach per gallon to treat the water.

Here in Arizona water is a precious resource and should not be taken lightly. If you live in a place like Washington State where it rains almost daily you can harness that and use the rain to have a renewable water supply. The rule of three is always in effect. Three minutes without air, three days without water and three weeks without food. This is what will kill you and the urban survivalist will not be conquered.

3) Food Storage

The next thing we need to cover is beginning to get stocked up with a short term and long term food storage. When we talk about short term food supply what is the time frame you think of, one week, three weeks or three months. Well the correct answer is three months. If something horrific happens in the United States that cause the complete stop of delivery of goods and services, well you be one of the people standing in a FEMA line to get a loaf of bread and braving possible riots. Or are you going to be safe in your home with a full belly and better off than 99% of the other people in this country.

As a society we live on fast food and most people go shopping every week because that is all they have in their home is a one week supply of food. If most of these people were to stop buying food and consume every morsel of food in their home, they may have two weeks' worth. I believe that they defiantly will not be eating healthy and nutritious food giving them the energy they need to get them through extremely hard times. The human body is a machine and can withstand a lot. However if that machine does not get fuel it stops no matter how big, strong or tuff it is.

In the late 1980's we all saw pictures of people inside the Soviet Union standing in lines that stretched for blocks. Most people stood in those lines not knowing what the line was even for. Most hoped for bread, flour or potatoes. When they got up to the front of the line and were handed a roll of toilet paper it was more than they had and they could use it but you can't eat toilet paper and survive.

● ЛЕТО-ОСЕНЬ 1990 ГОДА. ОЧЕРЕДИ - ЗА ВСЕМ. ...За мясом..

The Soviet citizens had to rely on their government to help them survive. I don't know about you but I am going to make sure my family and I are taken care of. So what happens when the government stops or cannot supply food to the masses? There could be massive riots and possible military action taken against the citizens. This is a worst case scenario but other countries have been through it and we are on track to civil unrest if the government continues to tax us and pass bills that remove our civil liberties.

We all need to establish food storage to protect ourselves and our families. The food storage can be done all at once or over time this just depends on you and your finances. Most of us have to start small and work up to three months worth of storage. My wife and I was able to get our short term storage through coupon shopping. It took us about 4 to 6 months to get our short term storage stocked up and used only a few extra dollars a week.

My wife joined a coupon club called Coupon Sense. The club allowed us to get multiple Sunday papers which have coupon packs for a discount and provided a website that showed what items you can get super cheap or free and at which store. One day my wife went shopping and came home with 22 bags of groceries and had paid a total of 7 dollars. She had saved over 200 dollars. In the bags were multitudes of can goods for our short term storage that she had gotten for penny's or even free.

When buying food remember to buy what you eat. If you don't eat Oysters don't store them just because they last a long time and are high in protein. If you eat beef stew buy beef stew and then write the expiration date on the label and stock the pantry with the closest expiration date to the front. I go by the saying "First in, first out". Continue to use and rotate through your short term food supply. As far as the expiration dates go I have eaten soups that were 4 years past the expiration date and it was still good. Use the expiration dates to know which one to use first but you don't have to throw it out because it's out of date.

Can food is great for short term storage. Most can goods have an expiration date about one or two years from the date you purchase them. Like I mentioned before I have eaten soups that had been expired for 4 years and it was still just fine. As long as the can is not dented or bulged out the contents should still be good. Tuna and canned hams seem to have some of the longest expiration dates. They are usually about 5 years out from the date you purchase it.

MRE's are considered short term food supply. A typical MRE has a shelf life of 5 years. The shelf life depends on temperature the MRE's are stored at. If you leave an MRE in a hot car where temperatures can reach 130-140 degrees here in Arizona the MRE's shelf life will be diminished greatly.

Most of the food that is purchased in cardboard boxes only has an expiration date of about 6 months to a year. The boxes will keep for about one year but then the content inside will become stale and taste bad. The enemy of food is oxygen. If your food is exposed to oxygen and sun light it oxidizes the food causing it to become stale. Most food packaged in boxes has a large amount of oxygen locked into the plastic bag with the product accelerating its demise.

Long term food storage mostly consists of staple foods such as rice, beans, wheat and oats. When these staples are packaged in sealed cans with oxygen absorbers they can last up to 30 years or longer. These cans can be purchased at survival stores or online at websites like ldscatalog.org.

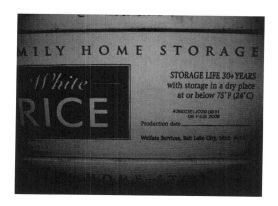

Dehydrated foods are becoming more available now and the cost is coming down. Even the big box stores like Costco are now selling dehydrated foods for emergency preparedness. Dehydrated foods are good for long term storage and you can store more in a smaller space. However one drawback is you need a lot of water to re-hydrate the food and if there is little or no water available then you have food but will be unable to consume it. If you start eating dehydrated food without water it could dehydrate you very quickly and make you sick. In a time of crisis, the last thing that you want to do is get sick.

During the great depression my grandparents did not have a refrigerator they had ice boxes. In the depression an ice box was exactly that, a box which held a block of ice to help keep things cold. Without a refrigerator or a freezer they could not keep meats, butter and milk very long. So they would pepper the meat and cut it into strips. Then the meat would be placed into a pillow case to keep insects off the meat and placed on a clothes line to dry.

After a full day of direct sun the meat would be jerky and then would be placed into a glass jar. The jerky could be eaten as is or cut up and put into a stew. Once in a stew the jerky would soak up the juices and re-hydrate making a nice juicy stew meat. In the old days my grandparents also made their own butter and made it so that it did not require refrigeration.

Beef jerky will last 2-3 years when packed into an air tight jar or container. It is not advised to package the jerky in plastic bags however. The plastic bags promote moisture and will slightly re-hydrate the jerky and shorten the shelf life. If you make jerky and vacuum seal your jerky and freeze it has the potential to last 5 years or more. Jerky can be a great benefit to your food storage. You can cut up beef jerky and put it in a soup. The boiling juices will re-hydrate the beef and provides your soup with a great flavor.

Canning can be very important when it comes to food storage. My grandma would can fruits and jams every year. There is something to be said about the taste of a homemade jam or jelly. No store brand can compare to homemade. Canning can be difficult and you have to know which of the two methods to can with. If you are interested in learning how to can your own fruits, veggies and meats it is advisable to get a good canning book and read it carefully. If canning is done improperly jars can break causing injury or bacteria can get into the jar and you or your family can get sick.

In your food storage I suggest to stock up on honey. Honey is the one of the only organic substances that will not spoil. Honey can be used as a sugar substitute and can be a comfort food in hard times. Honey over time may crystallize but once heated slightly it returns back to its original compound. Honey has been found in the ancient pyramids and after 3000 years it was still eatable and even reported to taste like fresh honey after being slightly heated.

Your food storage has several enemies; we have talked about oxygen being a primary enemy. The next enemy of your food storage is temperature. Your food will last a very long time if it is kept in a stable temperature such as inside your home between 70-80 degrees. If the temperature gets to high your foods shelf life will start to diminish. The last enemy of your food storage is sunlight. Sunlight promotes bacteria growth if it is able to shine on your food. This is way the Mylar bags work so well. They keep out sunlight and seals airtight.

Long term food storage can be overwhelming. Just look at your needs and find what works for you and your needs. There are many options and the one I use is to get a variety of goods that have been packaged in #10 cans and have a shelf life of 10 to 30 years depending on what has been packaged. There are a multitude of places these #10 cans can be purchased. I suggest going online and searching for a supplier. Try to find a supplier that is local to you so you can eliminate shipping by going there. Buying what you need locally can be beneficial because you can buy as little or as much as you want at a time.

Next is dehydrated foods these foods are good for long periods of time and I have even seen that after opening a can of dehydrated food it will still last 9 months to 3 years. However the drawback is water. Dehydrated food packs are light weight and easy to pack or carry and most will last 7 years plus. The water needed for each meal will add up significantly. When water is plentiful this may seem like the way to go. However think about this, if water is not flowing out of the tap and you need to ration water, this gives you an additional problem with a ration placed on food supply now due to your water situation.

The next thing to consider is turning short term storage into long term storage. This can be done by simply packaging your own staples.

Packaging your own staples: Staples are things such as rice, grains, wheat and beans. I have done this for myself and it is very easy to do.

This can be done easily by purchasing Mylar bags, oxygen absorbers and food grade 5 gallon buckets. These items can be purchased at www.preparingwisely.com now just follow these simple instructions.

First take inventory of what you want to package and make sure you have enough Mylar bags, oxygen absorbers and buckets.

Now I am going to package all of my store bought Oats into a 6 gallon Mylar bag and place it into a 5 gallon bucket.

Place the Mylar bag into the bucket and form it to the bucket. Then pour in the oats until you are about 2 inches from the top of the bucket not the top of the Mylar bag.

If you are packaging multiple items get everyone of them ready before opening your oxygen absorber package.

I packaged noodles into 1 gallon Mylar bags so that I can use smaller portions without having to expose all of the noodles at once.

A one gallon Mylar bag will typically hold 3 boxes of noodles or similar products.

At this point be sure to use a magic marker and write what you have put into the bag on the front of the Mylar.

Once you have gotten everything you want packaged ready, then pull out your clothes iron and set it for medium heat and let it warm up. Set out an ironing board or you can use a smooth piece of wood if you have to.

If everything is ready, then it is time to open the oxygen absorbers.

As soon as you cut the package you have a limited amount of time before the oxygen absorbers go bad. I use 2 to 3 oxygen absorbers per gallon of Mylar used. Now pull out the oxygen absorbers and place them into the bags. I try to spread the oxygen absorbers throughout the contents of the bag.

Now get your first bag and push as much air out of the bag as possible and hold the opening flat and use the iron to seal the bag. It is a good idea to leave one inch open in the corner and once again push out the excess air then seal the corner.

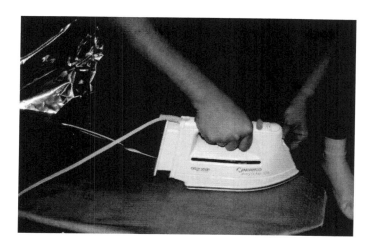

Now once you have completed sealing all of your bags fold the excess down into the bucket.

Once I was done with my Oats I still had about 4 inches of head space in my bucket so to maximize the space I added a completed bag of pasta wheels.

Once you have the Mylar folded into the bucket secure the lid onto the bucket and write the date and the contents on the lid of the bucket.

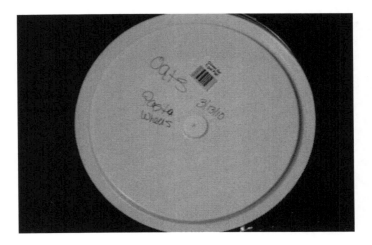

The Mylar will protect your food now for decades and the bucket protects the Mylar.

I went into Wal-Mart the other day and saw that they had a complete isle of long term food storage and water storage containers. I was glad to see that. Even the big box stores are trying to help people get prepared now, although they are just out to make money.

There are many different options of long term food storage. I cannot tell you which one is the best option because that depends on your needs and your environment. I suggest that you do some research for your area and get your food storage based on your needs and what you have available to you.

I also suggest that you purchase lots of olive oil. Not only can you cook with it, olive oil also burns as a clean candle fuel. You can float a wick in a jar half-full of olive oil and light the wick and you have a home-made candle. This candle works just as well as a Kerosene lantern. This will be covered later in chapter 7. Olive oil is a fantastic item for your storage anyway because even if you purchase all the grains in the world, you'll still need cooking oil. Well-stored olive oil can last for a thousand years as well.

Here is a quick tip. If you have wheat stored for future use you will be told that you need a wheat grinder to make flour. I can say you do not need a wheat grinder to make flour. You can use a normal blender to make flour. The only thing you have to do differently is add at least 2 cups maybe a little more to keep the wheat from flying up in the blender. If you don't have enough wheat in the blender the wheat will float up or fly around inside the blender and will not be processed into flour.

If you have a large amount of flour you have a few options to keep the flour safe from weevils. First is to keep the flour in the freezer this will kill any weevil eggs and keep new weevils from getting into the flour. If you are going to package your flour into Mylar bags for long term storage freeze the flour for at least 72 hours. Then package the flour with oxygen absorbers and a few bay leaves. This will protect your flour and keep it fresh for ten years or more as long as your flour has no yeast in it.

The second thing you can do is to place bay leaves in the flour and it will keep the flour safe for a year or so. After one year you should replace the bay leave with new ones. This is a short term storage idea. Even if you are storing flour the short term way buy a container that has an air tight lid to help keep weevils out and keeps the bay leaves fresher.

If you are in a survival situation and find that there are weevils in your flour supply there is something that you can do to save your flour. Simply pour the flour onto a cookie sheet and heat the flour to around 140 degrees. Stir the flour while it heats up. The heat will kill the weevils. After about 15 minutes at 140 degrees remove the flour and sift it to get out any weevils then repackage the flour. However it may be gross but eating a weevil never hurt anyone.

Quick Tip:

If you are in a situation in which you find yourself without power you can save your eggs from going bad. Coat the eggs in petroleum jelly. The jelly will stop the eggs from letting air through the shell and slows the aging process dramatically. The eggs should last for several months now.

When it comes to food storage, I always collect more than I think I could ever use. By doing this I have accomplished several things. First I will not go hungry in a desperate situation. Second if I have more food than I can use, I can barter food for other things I need. Third if any of the food that has not been used and is about to go bad then gets donated to the homeless shelters or orphanages so that it does not go to waste.

4) Personal Protection

There are several different levels and types of personal protection. Let's start with firearms. For personal protection it is recommended that you have three weapons. A handgun, a high powered rifle and a shotgun. The hand gun should be a common caliber like 9mm, 40 S&W or 45 ACP. The handgun is good for close range protection. The rifle again should be a common caliber like .223, 7.62X39, 270, 30-06, or .308. The rifle is used for hunting and long range shots that demand accuracy. The last must have weapon is a 12 gauge shotgun. If you are unable to get any other weapons it is advisable to at least get the shotgun.

The shotgun is a very versatile weapon. The shotgun can shoot multiple types of ammo and can cause devastating results. A slug fired from a typical 12 gauge shotgun is accurate and extremely deadly at 100 yards. Buckshot is a great personal defense round. Buckshot fires 9 .38 cal. lead shot and spreads at the rate of almost one inch per yard traveled. At 25 yards the 9 bullets would be in a 24 inch circle giving you a better chance of hitting and wounding your target. There is a new kind of Buckshot available that has a fluke wad. This wad slows the Buckshot expansion by half so at 25 yards your shot spread will be around 12 inches. Shotguns can also fire bird shot making it a food gathering weapon as well.

When it comes to buying the different types of ammunition for a shotgun the price varies greatly. If you were to buy 5 rounds of Buckshot it would be around five dollars or a dollar a round. Now if you buy a 100 pack of bird shot it will run you around 25 dollars. I suggest that you buy the 100 round pack and even if you don't have a reloader you can still make home defense rounds yourself.

First take a shotgun shell and a drill with a ¼ inch drill bit. Now drill a hole through the crimped end of the shell. Then pour out some of the shot and drop in several ¼ inch ball bearings or sling shot ammo. Once you get it up to the top you can pour in a few pieces of shot that you took out to fill any gaps. Then lastly reseal the end with some silicon. Silicon is flexible enough to allow the end to blow open when fired. Now you have a cheap and reliable home defense round.

With these firearms it is advisable to get into reloading your own ammunition. For reloading the shotgun I highly recommend the MEC 600 Jr. It is an awesome little reloader and only costs about $129 - $149 and is simple to use. Shotgun shells can be reloaded a dozen times or so making it cheaper than buying ammo. Also when loading shotgun shells you can put just about anything you want into the shell to shoot. If it is during dire times you can shoot rocks out of a shotgun although not recommended but you can.

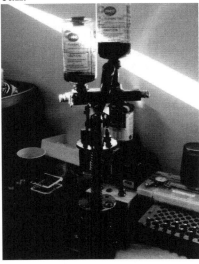

Next I would recommend the LEE Challenger press for reloading handgun and rifle ammunition. The kit cost around $100.00 and is a simple press and does a good job. The reloading process is a little slow with this single stage press but it gets the job done and doesn't break the bank. If you get into reloading I recommend getting a good reloading manual and take your time to learn the proper reloading techniques and procedures.

When it comes to personal protection I have prepared what I call Home Security and the three phases.

Home Security and the three phases

1) First phase includes the following:

- Walk around the house and look at the property and analyze every point of entry and look at different options for securing them.

- Next add locks to gates or storage containers etc. and buy good heavy master locks that are all keyed the same. This eliminates the need for multiple keys and the simplicity of having one key for access.

- Add a large hasp or lock to the middle of gate instead of the top of the side gate. By reinforcing the middle, the structural integrity of the gate is dramatically increased.

- Place a lock on your electrical box. If your power is shut off it can leave you with a tactical disadvantage.

- Add motion lights to exterior perimeter to give you the advantage of sight at night. If

you place the lights over a window you
can look out that window with some
privacy due to the light projected outward
takes sight from that location when
viewed from a dark distance.

- Make sure that your porch light is in an
  enclosed type fixture so an intruder can't
  remove or break the bulb before trying to
  make entry into your home.

- Check your garage door if you do not
  have a garage opener. Without an opener
  make sure there is a latch on both sides of
  the garage door. With only one side latch
  the door can be pushed to one side and the
  door will open. If you park outside your
  garage **NEVER** leave the garage opener
  in the car.

- Cameras are always a deterrent. It's not a
  bad idea to put one or two cameras on the
  front of the house and one in back.

- If you can get your hands on a security monitoring service sign post it out front even if you don't have an alarm.

- Clean out the garage and park the cars in there if at all possible. People who keep their cars in the garage usually have fewer problems with damage from an opportunist who saw something in your car they just can't live without.

- Get a good quality security door and keep it locked. Use the duel sided keyed dead bolt. You can keep a key on a hook by the door if someone comes over and your keys are in another room then simply use the key kept by the door. The key however needs to be somewhat out of sight from anyone at the door. Security doors are nice to have if someone is at the door you can open your front door and converse with the stranger without sacrificing too much security. That's also why the security door MUST stay locked at all times.

2) Second phase includes the following:

- Now move to the interior portion of the structure and look at every door and window to find any weak points.

- Buy wooden dowels and cut them to fit inside the window track in the bottom of the window frame to insure the window could not be opened even if left unlocked.

- Remove the ¾ inch standard screws that are in the door strikers and replace all screws with at least 2 inch screws or even 3 inch screws. This one trick can be the difference between a bad guy getting in or staying out.

- If there are windows beside doors which if broken give any intruder access by simply reaching in and unlocking and opening your door, change the dead bolt to a keyed deadbolt. This type of deadbolt requires a key to be opened from inside or outside.

- Also you can buy a $3.00 door stop form any home store and place it on the bottom of the door, once inside flip the door stop down and if the door is kicked open the door stopper can stop the door from opening more than a few inches.

- Think about tinting your windows. With tint the windows when broke stay together better and makes them stronger. Also it makes it harder for anyone outside to look in. Along with security you get an energy savings from the heat reflecting from the windows by tinting.

- There are small alarms that you can buy for several dollars that you can place on your doors and windows. These little alarms are placed on your door by adhesive tape on a door frame and the magnetic strip goes on the door. When armed and the door opens the alarm sounds. This will give any bad guys the appearance of a home alarm system and scare them away or alert you that someone is coming in.

- If you don't have the money for a video surveillance system then here is a tip. You can go to your local hardware store and buy a 200 degree peep hole. Next cut a 2X4 into a small square and drill a hole in the center of the board. Now drill the specified size hole in your garage door.

Place the new peep hole into the garage door with the wood block on the interior and tighten down the peep hole. You have just made a poor man's surveillance system. If you believe someone is outside your home or something is happening just walk into the garage and take a look. From my garage I can see the neighbor's driveways on both sides of me and the four homes across the street. The total cost of the project was $8.00.

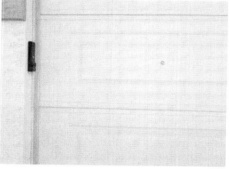

3) Third phase includes the following:

- For less than $1000.00 you can purchase two items. 1) A shotgun, I prefer the Remington 870 12 gauge pump shotgun. 2) A handgun, I prefer the Glock 22 40 cal. These are my preferences and you should shoot several different models before deciding on with weapon you feel comfortable with.

- If possible take a few handgun classes such as tactical handgun or tactical shotgun to learn all of the best techniques to better defend yourself.

- If you are the type of person that refuses to own a gun then please buy some pepper spray or a Tazer to help defend yourself.

- If you are still worried about bad guys entering through windows or doors then it is time to either make or buy window bars or steel storm shutters. I like the idea of welding several strips of flat steel together and place it into the interior side of the window and bolt it into the window frame as well as the studs. The steel can be painted or powder coated any color and can even be bent or twisted to give it an artistic or pleasant view. You can always purchase shutters or window bars from a reputable manufacture.

- With full glass or half glass doors you may want to add some flat steel to the door that prevents entry through the door if the glass is broken out.

- The front and back door can be extremely reinforced by placing steel brackets on the side of the doors and placing a 2x4 board across the door. With this in place the door cannot be kicked in AT ALL. This is the poor man's method. If you want a high priced pretty version check out ultimatelock.com.

- While inside your home think of a few
  scenarios. If someone were to come in
  while you are asleep and it woke you up,
  where do you go and what do you do. If
  you run the scenarios through your mind
  like this and it happens you will already
  have a plan and your reaction time is far
  better. This could be the difference
  between life and death.

- Look around the house and find a place to
  go to hide or make a stand. This could be
  your bedroom closet or the bathroom it's
  your house you will know where to go
  now fortify it. Place a door stop on the
  door and the poor man's door brace for
  the interior of the door is a good idea.

- If you pick a bedroom or a closet you can
  fortify the space and even make it safe
  from gunfire if you prepare it correctly.

- Once the safe room is selected hide a
  firearm in the room and out of the reach of
  any child. This can be done by many
  different means. I made a handgun holder
  by attaching a dowel to a small broad and
  screwing the board to the wall behind the
  clothes in the closet. Then I placed the
  barrel over the dowel. The dowel holds
  the firearm and it is up high away from
  little hands and hidden. You may even
  keep a firearm safe in the safe room for

easy access and storage. Make sure the safe can be opened fast but is inaccessible to children.

- Also to protect yourself from incoming gun fire you can get 2x6 lumber make multiple boxes 2 foot by 2 foot, secure ½ plywood on one side and silicon the inside. Place a 2 inch by 2 inch board cut to 5 ¾ inches long into the middle of your box and secure it to the plywood. Once the silicon is dry fill the box full with sand. Run a bead of silicon on the edge of the box and place a piece of 5/8 drywall on the box and screw it down on all edges and to the middle board and let the silicon dry. (The middle board is optional however it only helps to prevent the drywall from being pushed out under the weight of the sand). After you have made several of these you can place them into your safe room and place the drywall side to the interior of the room. Now you can tape and texture the boxes to look like part of the wall. A 2x6 board actually measures at 1 ¾ inches by 5 ¾ inches, so with 5 ¾ inches of sand it has been tested and will stop handgun rounds such as 9mm and 45 ACP. The boxes will also stop rifle rounds such as 5.56 (.223) and up to and including 308 cal. And even a 12 gauge slug fired at 25 yards away.

-

- Another technique that is very effective but is rarely used is to place a motion sensor flood light in a hallway or above a bedroom door. Once you are ready for bed you can turn on a switch and then if anyone enters the house and comes down the hallway the light turns on blinding and scaring the attacker and giving you the tactical advantage.

- With all the right security measures in place it is ideal that a firearm will never be needed. However we must be ready mentally to use one if that day comes.

- All these ideas can be expanded on or simplified. It is up to you and your security needs.

- It is your life you don't have to be paranoid, you have to be safe.

Home Invasion Statistics

Property Crime Facts (According to the FBI in the US: www.fbi.gov):

- One property crime happens every 3 seconds.
- One burglary occurs every 10 seconds.
- One violent crime occurs every 20 seconds.
- One aggravated assault occurs every 35 seconds.
- One robbery occurs every 60 seconds, or 1 minute.
- One forcible rape occurs every 2 minutes.
- There were over 2 million burglaries in 2005.
- An increase in burglary offenses was the only property crime to increase in 2005 compared with the prior year data.

Home Invasion Facts:

According to a United States Department of Justice report:

- 38% of assaults & 60% of rapes occur during home invasions.
- 1 of every 5 homes will experience a break-in or home invasion. That's over 2,000,000 homes!
- According to Statistics Canada, there has been an average of 289,200 home invasions annually over the last 5 years.
- Statistically, there are over 8,000 home invasions per day in North America

- According to Statistics U.S.A., there was an average of 3,600,000 home invasions annually between 1994 and 2000.

It's time to prepare yourself and not become a statistic, stop crime from affecting you, your home and your life.

Last but not least by preparing you can keep yourself and the ones you love safe from danger.

Don't be a victim it is your choice.

This Thief broke in using a screwdriver

Results of a Home Invasion

Common Tool used
by Burglars

Copper theft on the rise

These are everyday occurrences, now if you add a natural disaster or a massive terrorist attack you can bet the trials and tribulations are going to be ten times that of your worst day. If these three phases are followed and adapted, your exposure to crime or violence can be reduced greatly.

What I have seen year after year on the news that disturbs me is when hurricanes are headed for a certain location and you see people in a panic trying to cut wood for the windows and getting generators from Home Depot. You see the shelves in the stores cleared out of water, batteries and other essentials. I ask you, if you live in an area where you are at risk of hurricanes why would you not be prepared for them?

Even if you do not live in an area where hurricanes are a problem, there is always something that can affect you wherever you live. Be it tornados, micro bursts, winter storms, heat waves or floods. No matter where you live it is a good idea to have ¾ inch plywood cut to place over your windows in case of an emergency. This could even help you in a civil unrest situation. Most people live day by day. It's time for us to start looking to the future so we don't suffer in the present.

When it comes to personal protection it is also recommended that you obtain a gas mask for yourself and additional ones for anyone in your household. When purchasing a gas mask, you should purchase a high quality mask. The masks purchased at your local army surplus store may work but most are subpar and need to be inspected before purchase. If the mask comes with a filter installed on the mask it is no good. You will need to purchase new filters. The masks filter should be kept in the sealed bag they were shipped in due to the fact that the filters begin to filter air as soon as they are exposed to it. If the filters are removed from the package they are only good for several hours.

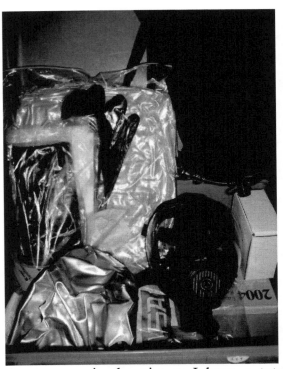

As you see in the picture I have a total personal protection kit. I hope that I will never have to use it but if the time comes I will be prepared. If you don't have the means to get a kit like this at least have some 3M N95 masks on hand to protect yourself or your family. These masks are disposable but have exceeded the standards set by the CDC.

5) Should I stay or should I go.

When it comes to a natural disaster, terrorist attacks or civil unrest you have to make the most important decision for your survival and situation. Do I stay or do I bug out. If you stay, you have to check your supplies and prepare your home for the worst. Do you have water, do you have electricity, and do you have safety. If you have applied the three phases of home security then you should have protection and be able to defend your property better than your neighbor.

If you are in a situation like hurricane Katrina you may need to bug out. When I say bug out I mean to get the hell out of dodge. If you are bugging out what do you take and where do you go. It is always good to make a plan and have a place to go. You would be surprised to find how many people have never thought about that. If you have to go make sure you have a list of supplies that you should take. Just remember you should have at the very least 72 hours of provisions per person in your household.

The urban survivalists should have a bug out bag in every vehicle and one in their home ready to go at all times. I know what you're thinking, what do you put in a bug out bag. Your bug out bag should be like your finger print. All finger prints have loops and swirls but the finger print is unique to you.

There are a few things that all bug out bags should have and that includes the following:

1) Matches, lighter or a fire starting devise.
2) Water, at least several bottles worth.
3) Food, MRE's,ER Bars or dehydrated food packets.
4) A tent or emergency blanket.
5) Rain gear.
6) A knife.
7) A multitool. (I.E. Leatherman)
8) Rope or Para cord.
9) A magnifying glass.
10) A first aid kit.
11) Several trash bags. (for getting water or improvised rain gear and keeping gear dry)
12) Water purifying tablets.
13) Razor blades.
14) LED Flashlight and batteries. (LED's last longer and use less battery power)
15) Crank flashlight radio.
16) One change of clothes.
17) Duct tape
18) Plastic sheeting
19) Zip lock bags quart size (perfect for storing food and keeping small items dry.
20) Toilet paper
21) Life Straw water purifier

Number 10 the First aid kit should contain the following:

1) CPR kit
2) Band aids
3) Gauze pads
4) First aid tape
5) Pack of sterile swabs
6) Cotton balls
7) Isopropyl Alcohol
8) Hydrogen Peroxide
9) Iodine
10) Hand sanitizer
11) Eye drops
12) Extra strength Motrin
13) Aspirin
14) Triple antibiotic cream
15) EPI pens (if you are allergic to something and have a need for the pen)
16) EMT shears
17) Tweezers
18) Matches or a lighter
19) Rubber tourniquet
20) Snakebite kit
21) Several 3M respirator masks
22) If possible several Quik Clot packages

Quik Clot has been used by the military to stop soldiers from bleeding to death when faced with a serious injury or gunshot wound. One Quik Clot package cost around $30 but to stop a major bleed it would be worth every penny to me.

The previous lists were the minimums for your bug out bag. Now here are few recommendations from the urban survivalist of what you could add beyond the minimums.

1) Water purifying filter system.
2) Fishing line (For traps, fishing or stitches)
3) Tin foil (multiple uses)
4) More toilet paper.
5) A hat to help keep the sun off your head.
6) Mosquito net. (Can be used for fishing as well)
7) Medicine.
8) Map of area bugged out to.
9) Plastic zip lock baggies. (Quart size seems to work best for most applications but add in a dozen gallon sized bags as well)
10) Water proof matches. (or take regular matches and dip them into finger nail polish, once they dry the matches will be waterproof)
11) Quick clot for first aid kit.

12) A roll of plastic sheeting. (More uses than I can list)
13) Roll of duct tape.
14) A handgun and as much ammo as you can carry.
15) A rifle or shotgun and as much ammo as you can carry.
16) Beef jerky (light weight and packed with protein)
17) A sharpening stone (A knife is only as good as its blade is sharp)
18) GPS

This is what I usually take with me. Now you should decide what you need for you and for your environment. The majority of the items in your bug out bag are small and light weight but are very valuable. The bulk of the weight will come from three items, food, water and ammo. This list can be looked at and then added to or subtracted from but as long as you have a bug out bag you are on your way to survival.

The next type of bug out bag that you need to consider is a bug out bag that stays in your car. Some people have never thought about this. If something happens and you are unable to get back home but you have your vehicle bug out bag then you should be ok for at least 72 hours.

This is a list of what the urban survivalist keeps in a vehicle bug out bag.

1) 2 two litter bottles of water. (Change the every 6 months)
2) 3 MRE's or dehydrated food packets. (These should be changed every two years due to the heat)
3) A change of clothes.
4) A complete tool kit.
5) Tow rope and tie downs.
6) A flashlight.
7) Toilet paper.
8) Duct tape.
9) A book of matches or a lighter.
10) A few trash bags.
11) A can of black pepper. (pepper will stop radiator leaks)
12) An extra engine belt.
13) Fix a Flat tire inflator slime.
14) A 12 volt tire inflator.
15) First aid kit. (Same contents as listed prior)
16) Rain poncho
17) Tri fold shovel (E Tool)
18) Try to always top off the fuel at a half tank.

As with the personal bug out bag this can be looked at and then added to or subtracted from, but have a plan and have the supplies on hand.

The last bug out bag that I want to introduce you to is what I call the ultimate bug out bag. One day I stumbled onto a 1978 Starcraft pop-up tent trailer for $500.00. I bought the trailer and put about $100.00

into it and got it up to par. The trailer has a 15 gallon water tank for water storage. It also has a battery for the interior lights along with a propane stove. I packed my trailer with everything I needed to survive. If anything ever happened I could simply hook up to the trailer and drive to my bug out spot.

Although I have the trailer you always need a back up. I have several 33 gallon Rubbermaid totes with all of my gear ready to go at any moment. In one of the totes I keep a 7 man tent. This tent can hold my family and my gear but it is small enough so it can be carried on a backpack if needed.

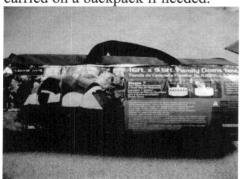

My bug out spot took me a long time to find and fits all of my needs. I measured my bug out trailer and found a spot that has four trees deep in the forest that I can pull my trailer between. The trees provide cover as well as stability in super high winds. I have already buried supplies in my bug out spot and have it prepped to be available at all times. I had even gotten another Fresnel lens and placed it in the trailer to cook with as to preserve the propane. I also know that if I have to bug out to the forest I have a homemade Just-In-Case book dedicated to the task of knowing what plants are editable and which ones are poisonous.

If something happens to the magnitude that you need to bug out, have a plan if you leave. Without having a plan or a specified destination you are setting yourself up for failure. I suggest that you get out a map book and find a spot within 2 to 3 hours from your current location and then go there to scout it out. Find a place off the beaten path and make it your own. You may even find a spot that will accommodate all of your needs and more.

When trying to find a bug out spot think of the year round conditions. Consider factors such as if it is winter time, is your bug out spot accessible. Depending on your location and circumstances you may want to find a couple bug out spots that could accommodate your needs at the time of the bug out. When looking at your bug out spot check and see if it is in a flood plain or if your potential bug out spot may lay on a fault line. If at all possible get off of the beaten path to minimize contact with other people or other people setting up in your chosen spot. These are things that should be considered.

Once a bug out spot is found you can prep your bug out spot by doing a few simple things. Build a fire pit that can allow you to cook and harness the heat of the fire. This can be accomplished by using rocks and one bag of cement to create a half moon circle. Now cement in a cooking rack about 12 to 18 inches off the ground. Level the bug out spot and clear away debris. Now before you leave the area you can use branches and hide your spot so that no one sets up camp in your bug out spot.

I have found a spot in the mountains that is away from any camp sites but only off the beaten path by a quarter of a mile. However this quarter mile is what separates me from the masses and is hidden out of sight and away from any roads. I made a path to my site and know how to get back there and I can say that no one will be in my spot if I need to bug out. I have even taken bricks and mortar to my site and made a huge fire pit. I have even gone as far as to bury some additional supplies in the ground at my bug out site.

You should always prepare beforehand. To get prepared I suggest buying several 33 gallon Rubbermaid totes. Then load the totes up with basic survival gear mainly consisting of camping supplies. If you decide to bug out then you all need to grab is food, water and your totes and bug out.

When it comes to urban survival or wilderness survival you have to beware of your surroundings and what resources you have at your disposal. Even in an urban environment there are editable and poisonous plants. If you find yourself in a bug out situation have an idea of what you can or cannot eat to help subsidize your limited food supply.

The decision to bug out or to stay at your home is the decision you and only you can make. Your decision will be based on the factors at hand and you should be willing to weigh all of your options very carefully before deciding.

If you bug out or not I want to show you something you should have at all times, an EDC kit. EDC or everyday carry kit can be as small as an Altoids can or a small fanny pack. No matter what you use it is a good idea to have something. I use a plastic box that measures 3 ½ inches by 2 ½ inches by ¾ of an inch.

My kit is the size of a medium sized cell phone but contains the following:

1) 3 feet of duct tape
2) 2 razor blades
3) 3 feet of dental floss
4) A buck knife with 2 blades
5) A mini Leatherman multi-tool
6) 3 6 inch zip ties
7) Water proof matches and striker
8) One foot square tinfoil
9) 6 feet of black tread
10) Pain medication
11) Allergy medication
12) Steel wool
13) P38 can opener
14) 3 rubber bands
15) 2 paper clips
16) 2 Band-Aids
17) 1 wet wipe

18) 3 feet of Para cord
19) 2 toothpicks
20) 3 inch saw blade
21) 1 large rubber glove
22) 1 safety pin

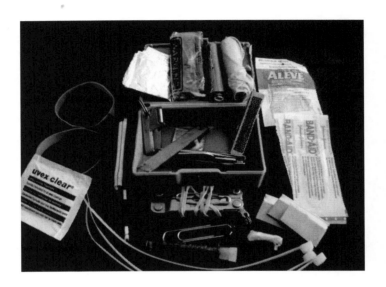

This kit has helped me on many occasions. The EDC kit is very important and should be a must for everyone. Depending on what size of container you use you can add to or take away from the list I have came up with. If you're a person who needs to carry inhalers or Epi pens then I suggest adding them to your EDC kit so that you will always have them.

Even if you decide not to bug out or have a bug out bag it is a good idea to at the very least have an EDC kit.

6) Survival garden

If you're not a green thumb type of person it might be time to try again. There is no better way to supplement your food supply than to have a garden. My garden is only about 8X12 feet but yields huge amounts of delicious veggies. I went to my local Wal-Mart and purchased a large amount of seeds. I then dug out some rolls and planted a bunch of various seeds. I added water and here in Arizona we have plenty of sunshine so then I just watched it grow. The garden soon became my stress outlet. It gives me a good feeling to do a little work and get a great tasting result. My garden has now turned into a pretty cool hobby.

I know some people who hate gardening and refuse to even have a house plant, but if you're reading this book you may want to revisit the gardening arena. If I can give you any advice I would say start small and work your way into it. If you live in an area where you do not have room for a garden or do not want to rip up your current backyard landscape then I have the solution, The Earth Box.

The Earth Box is a way to plant your favorite fruits or vegetables in a movable or transportable tub. The Earth box uses less water and yields high results. You can go on to Earthbox.com and look at these planting systems or you can make your own. If you are a little handy and have a few tools you can do this yourself for a few bucks vs. 50 dollars plus for one Earth Box.

A self watering container is a container that has a water reservoir built in. This reservoir waters the plants sometimes for several days. These containers can also contain a fertilizer band to feed the plants for the season. This makes the process of growing almost any flower or vegetable very easy to do and is very productive. Another advantage is it can be placed somewhere where there is no way to have a garden such as a deck or patio.

This will show you step by step how to make your own self watering containers. They are made using plastic storage tubs, 5 gallon buckets, small pots or planters although they can be made of other things as well (plastic garbage pails, laundry pails, Tupperware, Fancy planters, Cat litter pails, Etc. You only need 5 parts the container usually a tub or a bucket, the aeration screen, supports for the aeration screen, a fill tube, and a mulch cover. I will show you the method for making this container. The focus of this chapter is to be able to make these containers as cheaply as possible but still be functional. In the next section I will discuss each piece in more detail and show you each component of the design.

The container

The container can be just about any kind of tube or bucket that has enough room for the dirt or potting soil for the type of plant that you want to grow. Vegetables seem to be the popular use but you can use the container for just about any type of plant. The container is divided into two parts the soil camber and the water reservoir. The two compartments are separated by an aeration screen. The container has a hole drilled just below the aeration screen as an overflow so that the container cannot flood. Most containers like the one in the pictures to follow are made from plastic storage tubs.

The aeration screen

The aeration screens purpose is to separate the soil chamber from the water reservoir and hold the soil above the water giving oxygen access to the root system. The aeration screen has multiple holes in it allowing the dirt access to the water. Once the dirt touches the water it now acts as a wick and the water will actually travel up through the dirt supplying the plant with the proper amount of water. Aeration screens are made from another tub exactly like the container and a few pieces of PVC which is called the screen supports.

The screen supports

The screen supports main job is to hold up the aeration screen and act as a wicking chamber. The support are anywhere from 3 to 5 inches in height depending on the size of the container. The supports should have a bunch of holes drilled into the sides all the way around the PVC pipe. The holes in the pipe allow water and oxygen to enter the soil and root system of the plants. The holes at the top of the PVC will be used to secure the PVC to the aeration screen with tie wraps or nylon wire.

The fill tube
The fill tube will be the PVC pipe that extends out of the top of the container and has only one purpose. It is the means in which the water is introduced into the container without pouring it directly onto the soil.

The mulch cover
The mulch cover will be made out of thick plastic and is secured to the top of the container by the lid after the center has been cut out. The plastic should vary depending on your climate. If it is hot outside then you should be using white or clear plastic. If it is cold or winter time then thick black plastic should be used to absorb the suns heat.

Poor man's Earth Box design

I will show you a design that you can make cheap
and easy. Remember that you can use almost
anything as long as it can perform the same function
as the parts I show you in this section. You can use
the same type of product as shown or you can come
up with your own version. Get creative and see what
you can do.

This design requires two storage tubs. The idea is that
the bottom of one of the tubs is cut off and
transformed into the aeration screen for the container
tub. This method does have an additional cost due to
the fact that you need two storage tubs.

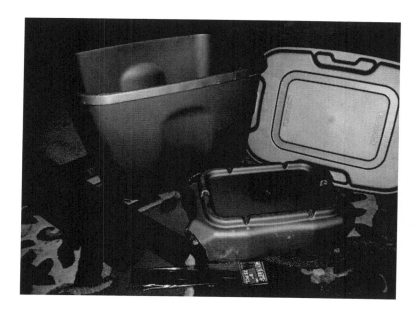

The materials that I used for this project include the following:

Two 10 gallon storage tubs.
1 foot section of 3 inch PVC for wicking chambers
2 feet section of 2 inch PVC for water fill tube
8 zip ties

You can use larger tubs or wider tubs and different wicking chambers and sizes of PVC. This is what I used not what has to be used.

First I measured one of the tubs and drew a line 3 inches from the bottom all the way around the tub. Them I cut off the bottom of one of the tubs at the three inch mark. Most storage tubs can be cut with a razor blade or knife. Make sure to cut the bottom straight so that it will lay into the bottom of the container flat. Once the bottom is cut you may have to touch up the cut. Find a flat surface and lay the cut portion upside down to check if it is level.

Placed the cut portion upside down and locate where
you want the wicking chambers to go. Also find a
place to cut out a circle for the 2 inch PVC fill tube.

Using the 3 inch diameter PVC, cut the section into 3 inch long wicking chambers. Once you have cut the PVC drill multiple holes into it, this allows the wicking process to occur.

To finish the aeration screen now drill multiple holes
into the bottom of the screen. This helps oxygen and
more water gets to the roots.

Be sure to drill four holes close to the top of the PVC
and attach the PVC to the aeration screen using the
zip ties.

Next locate a corner where you want to place the fill tube. Cut out the corner so that the fill tube will be held tightly and be unobstructed to the bottom of the container.

Place the completed aeration screen into the container and drill a over flow hole just below the top of the aeration screen.

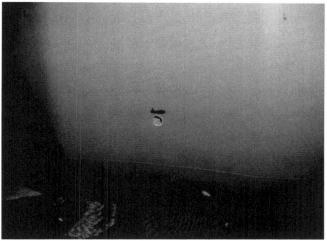

Last cut the middle out of the lid and cut a hole for the fill tube. Be sure to take care to cut the fill tube hole in the proper location so that the lid will fit properly and will not be strained. If the lid does not fit properly then the plastic cover will not stay tight or may fly off in the wind.

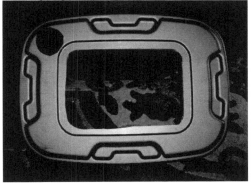

When done your portable planter should look
something like this.

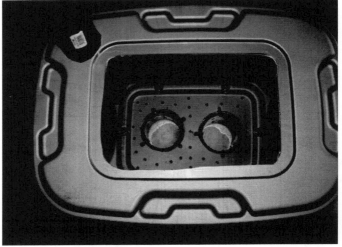

Now just add soil, fertilizer and seeds. Fill the
reservoir with water until it comes out of the over
flow and place a trash bag over the top with an X slit
over each seed planted and you're on your way.

This is one of my first planter boxes that I made. The
radish's had come up in record time and were ready
to eat sooner than the ones I planted in my garden.
This allowed me to pull them and replant Okra. The
two Okra plants I planted in the planter box out
preformed four other Okra plants that I had also
planted in my garden.

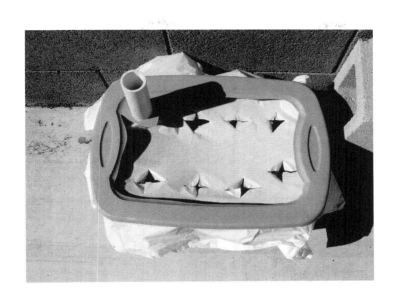

Setting up the container for planting:

1. Place the container where you are going to keep it. Put your container in a sunny spot that gets 6 to 8 hours of sun per day. Once you fill the container they become very heavy and difficult to move so it is best to place it in its final location before you fill it.

2. Get a bucket or other suitable container to moisten the initial potting mix. Make sure that it is moist but not soaking wet. Use this first potting mix to fill the wicking chambers. After you fill the wicking chambers you can pour the potting mix directly into the container and moisten with water. Fill the water reservoir with water through the fill tube until water comes out of the overflow hole.

3. Continue adding moist potting mix on top of the screen until the container is half full. It's OK for some of the mix to fall through the screen. Sprinkle the potting mix with water and gently pat it down, especially above the two wicking chambers you filled first.

4. Fill the container completely to the top with potting mix. Do not leave a space along the sides. Again sprinkle well with water and smooth the soil to the top edges, leaving a slight mound down the center. For tomatoes, mix two cups of dolomite or hydrated lime into the top 3-4 inches of potting mix and re-smooth.

5. Pour two cups of dry fertilizer in a 2" wide stripe directly on top of the potting mix. DO NOT MIX THE FERTILIZER INTO THE POTTING MIX OR

SPREAD IT AROUND. Simply pour it in a narrow strip on top and gently pat it down. Do not use fertilizer that requires mixing with water, such as Miracle-Grow™ or other "blue water" brands.

6. Place the mulch cover over the container and cut the hole for the fill tube. Pull the mulch cover down over the top of the container and secure with the lid rim or you can wrap a bungee cord around the container to hold the cover if needed. Some people in windy areas also tie two cords completely around the container as extra insurance. **Note: in hot climates you should try to use light colored plastic because dark plastic will heat the soil too much.**

7. Cut 3 inch X pattern in the plastic where the plant needs to go. Dig 2 to 3 inch deep holes into the potting mix (though the cover), just as you would in the ground. Place the plants or seeds in the holes and firm the mix around the roots. Just this one time, "water the plants in" from the top to remove any air spaces from around the roots and put the flaps back around the stems.

8. Your self watering container has all the fertilizer it needs for one complete growth. Always keep the cover on and keep the reservoir full by adding water through the fill tube until it runs out the drain hole. To replant, remove the old cover and dig out the fertilizer stripe. Top it off with potting mix, being

sure it is completely wet throughout, and add a new fertilizer strip. Install a new cover and plant again.

If something bad happens and you are forced to bug out you now have the option to take your garden with you. If you have any questions you can go on the internet and check out Earthboxresearch.com for information. You can see additional plans for multiple types of containers in full at www.seattleoil.com/Flyers/Earthbox.pdf

It is a good idea to start stocking up on seeds now. I would suggest that you get a bag or a Tupperware and start placing the seeds inside whatever type of storage container you have and place the container into the freezer. Once you place the seeds into the freezer they go dormant. If you leave the seeds anywhere else the seeds will go bad after one to two years.

The freezer helps preserve the seeds for years and is part of their natural cycle as well. Once you plan to plant your seeds, remove them from the freezer let them defrost and plant them. The seeds come out of a dormant state just as they were coming out of winter. If the governments of the world are storing seeds and putting them in a huge freezer, then maybe we should be doing it as well.

The Svalbard Global Seed Vault opened on February 26th, 2008 in Norway and holds approximately 1.5 million seed samples of agricultural crops are thought to exist. This vault is also called the Doomsday

Vault. The vault was built to withstand every natural disaster known to man including to stay out of water if the polar ice caps were to melt. It is very interesting and I would recommend that if you are surfing the internet one day check it out.

If you go on the internet you can order a seed package kit called The Ark.

The Ark contains all of your major vegetables to provide a nice sized garden. All of the seeds in The Ark are non hybrid seeds and will produce vegetables that have fertile seeds that can be used to plant more plants. If you buy seed packages at a store just remember to try and stay away from hybrid seeds. Some hybrid seeds will not yield healthy plants from the vegetables seeds.

If you start a garden it might be a good idea to also set up a rain barrel system to collect water to help water the garden and help with the water bill. Places like Arizona where we are in a drought it helps a lot. Also if you find yourself in the middle of a bad event you already have a water collection system in place. Although the water that you collect should be filtered or distilled it is water.

Your rain barrel doesn't have to be anything fancy it just needs to hold water and have a way to get the water out. With my rain barrel I used a water facet at the bottom of the barrel that I can simply attach a water hose to and run it out to the garden to water the plants.

I also placed the barrel on the north side of the house because it is in the shade all day long. When your barrel is in direct sunlight the water will grow algae and clog up the facet. If you have to place the rain barrel in direct sunlight it is a good idea to cover the barrel or use dark barrels to minimize the algae growth.

7) Urban Survival without grid tied power.

Let's say that something happens like a pandemic, civil unrest or god forbid another terrorist attack. If utilities fail and you decide to stay put, then there are some things to think about and take into consideration.

If there is a full meltdown and now you're stuck with a freezer full of meat, chicken and others what do you do? This depends on the time of year. If it is winter then you can set out bowls of water and make your own ice blocks to keep everything cold.

If it is summer time then the first thing you should do is start cutting meat into strips to be dried into jerky. The meat can be peppered and hung out in a pillow case to dry in the sun. The pillow case keeps the bugs off of the meat. Once it is done it can be stored for a year or more. However try not to store the jerky in plastic bag because the can promote moisture rehydrating the meat. If the bags are vacuum sealed the jerky will be fine and last longer. It you believe that the temperatures outside are just a little too low then use a solar oven or a grill and get the meat cooked or dried.

Second if you have a generator I suggest that you run the freezer on the generator for at least one hour a day. You should be able to run the refrigerator twice a day and keep things from spoiling. By keeping the refrigerator and freezer closed as much as possible the food should stay cold or frozen buying you time to ration your food supply.

Now if you run the generator outside you could run the risk of becoming a victim because it signals that you have power. To a bad guy if you have more than he does and he knows it, he is going to try and take it. The Urban survivalist can bring his generator inside the house or garage and runs a hose from the exhaust to the dryer vent or out the garage door. Caution: never use a generator in an enclosed area without ventilation. If you decide to use your generator outside be sure to lock it up.

With a 5000 watt generator you could run most refrigerators and freezers along with some lights. Just remember if you run the generator at night and use your lights, you might as well put a neon sign up saying come rob me. Be smart and black out windows when you use your resources. Do not let anyone know what you have or what you can do.

It might be advisable to look into a getting a small solar panel system. At Harbor Freight Tools they sell a small solar panel system with a control box and lights all for around $200.00. This is a start but it is low voltage and inefficient for most appliances. The system that you put together is going to be unique to your needs and might require a specialist in the solar field. Another thing to look into is wind generation. However if someone notices your solar panels or a wind generator they could target you for your resources.

When you are without power in the middle of the summer, the heat can be dangerous. If you have water available then there is a natural way to keep cool. Walk outside and lick your finger and hold it up in the air. You will feel which way the wind is blowing even if the air seems still, there is always movement. Go inside your home and open a door or window on the side of the house that the wind is blowing up against.

Next soak a towel or sheet and put it over the window or door. Now open a window or door on the opposite side of the house. You have now made a cross draft natural swamp cooler. The air will be pulled inside the house through the wet sheet and cool the incoming air up to 20 degrees or more. If water is being rationed you can use gray water to keep the sheet wet. Gray water is water such as dish water, bath water or water that is not drinkable.

If you have access to a solar panel then you can make a solar powered swamp cooler. Using an ice chest cut a hole in the side of the cooler. Then cut two smaller holes in the other side. Place an A/C vent filter or a towel in the middle of the cooler standing upright. Get a small submersible pump and put it in the cooler and run the discharge hose to the top of the filter or towel.

Place a fan in the bigger hole you had cut in the side of the cooler. You can get car air vents from a junk yard and place them in the smaller holes to direct the air. Then use the inverter that is powered by your solar panel and plug in the fan and pump and you have a homemade swamp cooler.

If it is winter time then you need to know how to stay warm. Have you seen a homeless person sleeping under news papers or in a cardboard box? They have learned those paper products are great insulators. If you have to bug out or get caught away from home without proper clothing, then try to find a cardboard box and crawl in there and line your clothes with news paper or magazine pages to keep warm.

If you are in your home with no power and you do not have a wood burning stove, there are still ways to stay warm. First pick a small room in the house that gets the most sunlight during the day and start preparing it. First cover the windows and A/C ducts with plastic. This is where 50% of cold air seeps through.

Now get every blanket, sheet and towel to line the room. Once inside the room, roll up a towel and place it at the bottom if the door to eliminate any drafts coming in.

During the day remove any blankets from the window to allow as much sunlight in as possible to help warm the room. If you have tin foil you can take it and put it on cardboard and place it at a 45 degree angle around the outside of the room's window. This will direct more sunlight into the room increasing the temperature dramatically. Make sure that you keep the whole family in one room. The more people you have in a small space the warmer the room will stay.

There are small emergency blankets that you can by in the camping section of Wal-Mart for $2.00. If you incorporate the emergency blanket into your situation you will be even better off. Never burn a fire or propane stove in an enclosed room; you could die from carbon dioxide poisoning.

If you want to make a solar heater here is a simple one to build. Start by finding a road side political sign which is constructed from corrugated plastic similar to cardboard. Now get some wood and cut a grove in the wood to slip the sign into the grove. Drill out a one inch hole into the board so that it connects with the grove. Now do the same for the other side of the sign. Paint the whole top of the board black, this will absorb a vast amount of heat from the sun.

Using a generator or an inverter powered by solar panel, hook up a shop vac on reverse so that it is blowing air into the wood. The air will disperse to the corrugated slots and will travel down the length of the board heating the air. Once it comes out the other side harness the air into a hose to be pumped into the house. Cardboard will work as well but is not water proof like the plastic sign board. Using this method on a 60 degree day, the sign board heater yielded 138 degree air at the discharge port.

If you have a fire place or BBQ and do not have fire wood there is an alternative. If you take news paper and roll it up as tight as possible and put duct tape around it and soak the paper in water then let it dry out in the sun you have now made a paper log. Once you burn the paper log it will burn for about 20 minutes. However beware if you are burning the paper logs outdoors and you have a breeze present, ambers from the paper can be blown up into the air causing a fire hazard.

Next let me introduce you to the Fresnel lens. I was able to purchase a broken 52 inch big screen TV on craigslist for 20 dollars. I then removed the Fresnel lens and the mirror in the back of the TV and threw away the rest. I then built a stand and put the lens in a frame ready to harness the power of the sun. Fresnel lens can also be purchased online for less than a hundred dollars. These lenses come in all sizes but bigger are better. If you have reservations because of the size, just remember the lens are only as thick as a piece of cardboard and can be stored behind a dresser or under a bed. The Fresnel lens is a great tool and in my opinion should be a must for the urban survivalist.

Without power it becomes more difficult to cook or boil water to drink. This is where the mighty Fresnel lens comes into play. As explained before you can use a metal container and ¼ inch copper tube to distill non potable water to make fresh water.

Now with the Fresnel lens you can also place a pot or skillet on a rack about 10 inches above a mirror and bounce the beam off of the mirror to the bottom of a pan and cook as if it were on a stove. I have even flash cooked a steak in a skillet by placing it in the focal point of the beam.

The Fresnel lens is an extremely powerful piece of survivalist equipment. It can cause a piece of wood to smoke and then burst into flames within 3 seconds.

It takes 787 degrees to melt a penny. When I tried to melt a penny, I only left half of the penny in the focal point for 30 seconds.

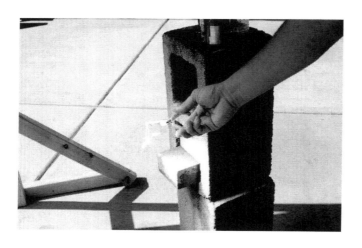

The results after 30 seconds of exposure to the power of the Fresnel lens proved to be too much for the copper coated zinc piece also known as one cent. If you look close you can see the tip of the pliers got hot enough to turn red and then discolored the hardened metal.

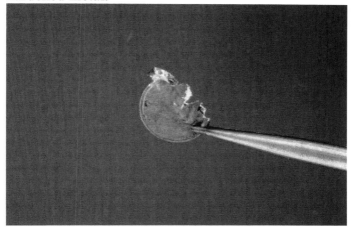

As you can see the power of the Fresnel lens is awesome and all that is needed is sunlight. This one piece of equipment can be adapted to hundreds of uses the only limit is your knowledge and imagination.

If you find yourself in a survival situation and are without a Fresnel lens then there may be an alternative solution. If you have a small satellite dish on your house you can use it to act a parabolic mirror to cook or heat. To accomplish this simply remove the dish off of the roof and remove the hardware from the dish. Then cut tinfoil in to 2 inch strips long enough to cover the diameter the dish. Glue the strips of tinfoil onto the dish with the duel side down.

Try to keep the tinfoil as flat as possible and free of wrinkles. Once you have covered the front of the dish you can start using it. Simply place the dish in the sunlight and using a wood stick you can find the focal point. Using tinfoil may only yield a focal point with a temperature of 500 degrees. If you are able to remove the paint on the dish and polish the metal to a mirror shine you can yield high results of around 2000 degrees from the dish.

If you're looking to cook or heat something and need 250-400 degrees for a long period of time. Then I suggest that you purchase a solar oven. I have seen these in action and they work phenomenal. With a solar oven you can bake bread or boil a stew. As long as the sun is out you can cook all day long without any power. I enjoy using mine out camping. It is easy to set up and easy to use, simply unfold the wings or flaps and insert food then face it towards the sun. There are several websites that have full plans to build your own solar oven out of cardboard, tin foil and a piece of glass.

The one I built cost me about $2.00. Here are the plans to make your own. You can always change it to fit your needs so have fun.

A solar oven can be a very simple thing to make. You can make a cheap and functional oven as simple or as a high-tech as you want.

You can probably make a solar oven from items that you already have around the house.

You will need the following:

1) Cardboard boxes in various sizes
2) Glue that holds good to paper and cardboard and is heat tolerate.
3) A large roll of tin foil.
4) A piece of glass.
5) Black BBQ paint.
6) Cotton cloth and string.
7) Finally a pan, can or small cookie sheet that will fit into the completed oven.

First, if for some reason you do not have any cardboard boxes around your home then you can go to your local grocery store and ask for some boxes. Most stores will give you all the boxes you can haul away. I recommend that you try to get square boxes. By getting square boxes you can get away from cutting a rectangle box and making your own square box.

You will need two square boxes one bigger and one smaller. The smaller one will need to fit inside the bigger one and this will be the cooking space. The larger box should be about 1 to 2 inches bigger in all directions. For a medium sized cooking space it should be around one foot by one foot and about a foot deep.

Cut several pieces of cardboard to fit inside the larger square oven box to boost the smaller square box up about one inch from the bottom and leaving it one inch lower than the top of the larger outer square cardboard box.

The larger outer cardboard box needs to have the flaps tucked in between itself and the smaller inner box. The inner box should have all of its flaps folded so that they are in between the two boxes as well. Now cut additional cardboard pieces and place them in between the two boxes until the smaller cardboard box is totally wedged in place. I placed all of the additional cardboard pieces in the larger box and then folded the flaps over them this helps lock all the pieces in place.

The lip of the smaller inner box is what will be holding in the glass, so take care to do a good job fitting the inner box so that the glass will be seated properly. If there are any gaps between the cardboard and the glass, heat will escape and your oven will not operate to its fullest potential.

Now paint the inside of the inner box black and put it aside to let it dry as you start on the collectors.

If you have stayed with these instructions then you have used square boxes. By using square boxes all four collectors will be the same size and once you make one you can use it as a template for the next three.

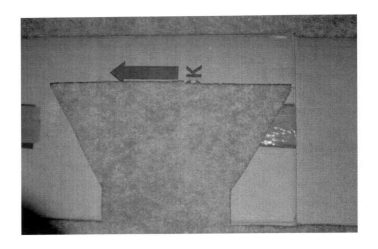

When making the collectors you will need four of them. The four collectors will be made from large pieces of cardboard measuring 2 feet by 3 feet each.

Once you have cut out your collectors draw a dotted line about 3 inches from the bottom. Now use a screw driver or butter knife and crease the cardboard along the dotted line. Now fold the bottom flaps of cardboard down. The four bottom flaps need to match each other so that your collector will sit properly on the oven.

Now glue the side flaps of the collectors together. Be careful that the collectors are maintaining a 67 degree angle. To give the collectors a little added strength you can poke holes and used string also tie the flaps together after gluing. This is advisable if the oven is going to be used during windy days.

As soon as the glue dries then it is time to glue the tinfoil on. I have found that if you use a mixture of two parts water and one part white glue it seems to work very well. Next spread the glue over the dull side of the tinfoil. Now place the tinfoil over the collector and try to keep it smooth. Be sure to press on the edges and pull out any big wrinkles. Use a towel or cloth and rub the tinfoil outwards to the edges to smooth it out.

Tin foil is hard to keep from wrinkling. Here I used dollar store tin foil and still achieved 200 degree temperatures. Higher quality tinfoil will be thicker and wrinkle less giving you a better mirrored surface and generate higher temperatures. It will still do the job but if you are able to use Mylar or mirrored tint it is easier to handle and will give you better results.

To attach the collectors to the oven box there are many different ways. I chose to use a slip-in piece. I did this by taking the bottom of the finished collectors that is extended downward 3 inches below the tin foil and place them between the inner and outer boxes of the oven. This makes the collector removable and easier to store. If you want to make it permanent then simply glue the collector into place.

If you do not have a piece of glass handy then I have a quick tip. Cut out a cardboard frame that will fit your opening. Then use a piece of plastic and cover the frame or like I did here, place the frame inside of a one gallon zip lock baggy and place it over the opening.

If mounting a metal rack it is a good idea that the rack pan or metal sheet puts a slight amount of pressure on the sides. This will help hold the inner box in place for stability. You can also make a rack or boil over pan from cardboard, wood or sheet metal. Now you are ready to use your solar oven.

On the first couple uses the oven may smoke as it heats up. This is called the curing process and will not hurt the oven; however as cardboard heats up it shrinks slightly. It is a good idea to check your inner box and add more cardboard on the sides for stability if necessary.

Once you get an empty vegetable can or coffee can I suggest that you paint it black and use the can to cook with. The metal will heat up and help cook food and heat better.

How to use the oven.

Using jars to cook can be simple. You can use boil or steam food in a recycled jar. Use only half gallon or smaller sized jars. The cooking time using these jars can also be reduced by painting the jar black. It is advisable to leave a small strip clear to see the food in the jar. When cooking be careful not to over fill the jars with food that expands such as rice and beans. Depending on what you are cooking it may be a good idea to poke a hole into the lid to release any pressure buildup.

Cooking with a solar oven is different than cooking with a conventional stove. There will be somewhat of a trial and error period. It is recommended that you use your solar oven so that you are proficient with it if the time comes when you need it. With that said here are a few tips.

Bread: When cooking bread get a one pound coffee can and let the dough rise slowly in the heat of the day then place the can into the solar oven and bake.

Beans and rice: When cooking beans or rice you should use about 2 ¼ cups of water to 1 cup of beans or rice. Once the beans or rice cooks and boil for a long period of time you may need to add an additional ½ cup of water.

Vegetables: most veggies will cook with very little water or a small amount of butter. It is a sign that the veggies are done as the veggies began to shrink in size.

Times of cooking will very due to the oven alignment and ambient temperature of the outdoors. Simply check on you food periodically and find the pattern for your oven and climate.

Now if you don't think you could build this project or need something simpler then here is a quick idea. First go to your car if you have a reflective sunshade then get it out. Next fold two bottom ends together and use a stick to keep the top open. This creates a bowl shape. Find a small wire rack and place it into the bottom of the bowl. Finally get a black pot and fill it with the food you want to cook or water you want to boil and then place it into a clear plastic bag and set it on the rack. You have just made an Urban Survivalist solar oven. The max heat expected out of this type of oven is 250 degrees however it will work. It will take 2 hours or more but it will boil water or cook food.

If you have kids then use the plans provided for a solar over or get a book on how to build one and let your kids help you. It will be a fun and a good learning experience for the kids and then you have a great piece of survival equipment. By showing the kids how to do these things you are also preparing them in case something god forbid happens to you, your kids will have a better chance to survive in any situation.

If you find yourself in a situation where you cannot make a solar oven then there is a quick alternative. If you have a reflective car shade you can make a solar oven in under a minute.

First fold out your sunshade with the cut out for the rear view mirror on the bottom.

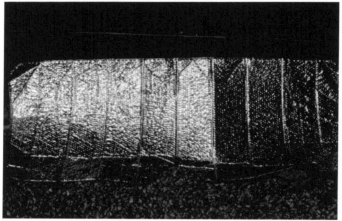

Next fold in both bottom corners bringing them together and place a rock in the pocket to hold the oven down.

Now place a pot with your food in a plastic bag and place it in the middle of the oven.

This solar oven will not reach boiling temperatures however it will heat food and cook food that only needs to reach pasteurization temperatures which is around 165 degrees. The oven can reach high temperatures when used with mirrors to reflect more light onto the object that needs to be heated.

A professional solar oven will cost between $250 and $400, I have built a quality solar oven that will sustain 350 degrees all day long. The materials were purchased at my local hardware store for about $130. This was a difficult project but not impossible. I started by building a wooden box with no lid. I then lined the interior of the box with 2 inch Styrofoam.

Next I made an inner box out of sheet metal and placed it into the box. I then cut the sun collectors out of sheet metal and attached them to the inner sheet metal box.

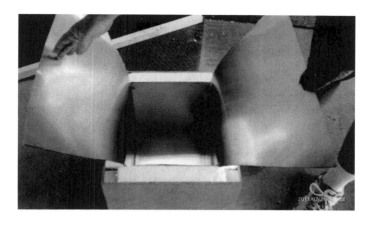

It is crucial that you maintain a 67 degree angle to keep the sun focused on the center of the oven. Once all four collectors are in place use ½ inch aluminum angle and secured the sun collectors together and made a top frame to give the collectors some support.

Next I used the aluminum angle, to make a frame for the door. I secured the frame to the top of the interior sheet metal box and attached the glass to the frame. Then I used food safe barbeque paint and painted the interior sheet metal box black. This helps to absorb more and maintain more heat into the box. I also installed an oven thermometer inside the box.

The last thing I did was used Silver Mylar and spray adhesive and covered the sun collectors. This gave the collectors a very reflective surface.

This oven heats up to 350 degrees in about 45 minutes and maintains that temperature for most of the day with minimal adjustments.

If you need to cook for a long period of time here is a very energy efficient way. You can use the power of the sun with a Fresnel lens, solar oven or even use a propane grill and bring your food to a boil. Next you can use 2 bean bags or thermal sleeping bags to keep the pot boiling for hours. Once you bring your food to a boil for at least 5 minutes then place one bean bag or sleeping bag into the bottom of a large Tupperware and place your pot into the middle of the bag.

Next place the second bag on top of your pot and tuck in all of the sides. You have just made a wonder box. I have done this and left my food to cook for up to 8 hours in the wonder box. When I removed my pot the contents were fully cooked and still steaming hot. This method is very simple and very effective.

The next thing I want to introduce to you is a little devise called an inverter you can buy them for $100.00 to $500.00 and it can power a few small appliances. You can purchase a 12 volt power inverter that plugs into your cigarette lighter in your vehicle. Inverters can range from 200 watts to 4000 watts. Simply plug in your inverter and plug in the devise you want to power. Periodically you need to start the vehicle to charge the vehicle battery so that the vehicle battery is not discharged to the point that your vehicle is now disabled and will not start.

The bigger inverters like the 4000 watt inverter can be used the same as the generator. As long as you have a battery and a way to keep it charged such as a small solar array, you can run just about anything you want. I have a 300/600 watt inverter and it will run a TV and a DVD player with no problem. I have ran a small refrigerator and then a computer all without fail.

There are other ways to make electricity which includes wind generation. If you live in an area where wind is abundant then you may consider a small wind generator. These can go anywhere from $600 to thousands. The small ones for under $1000.00 can power small appliances and lights when your power is out. They can be a great addition to a solar array as well. This may not be for you but it should be a consideration and "Green Projects" usually can be written off in taxes.

When using wind power you will most likely also have a battery bank to store your electricity. It is advisable to get a solar trickle charger for those non windy days; at least your batteries will receive a small charge. Even if you are using one battery to power an inverter a solar trickle charger could make the difference between power and no power.

For people in apartments or the like, there is a little thing you can do to charge a car battery and or power an inverter. If you have a bicycle then you can get set up to produce electricity. You can make your own if you are a bit of a handyman or you can spend a few hundred dollars for a Pedal-A-Watt type of bike stand. By doing this you can't power a whole lot but you can charge up and run small devices that do not have a large draw. These plans to do it yourself can be found on the internet.

I have seen a homemade generator made of a car alternator and a lawnmower engine. It is a simple project and if you are a do it yourselfer you could make one in a few hours. A friend of mine took a down shaft Honda lawnmower engine and mounted it to a piece of plywood and adapted a V-belt pulley to the shaft. He then mounted a car alternator with the pulley down to the plywood. The plywood is mounted on two 4x4 boards holding it off the ground giving the pulleys clearance to run.

He then connected the engine to the alternator with a standard alternator V-belt. The alternator was then connected to a standard car battery and an inverter was connected to the battery. With the engine running the alternator was putting out 13.8 volts and only dropped to 13.4 when the inverter was loading the battery.

The inverter ran small appliances, lights and a bunch of little gadgets making it a valuable asset. The engine came out of a broken lawnmower that was given to my friend and the alternator came off a junk GM car. He already had the inverter and bought a new battery for the project for fifty dollars. The final total was $50 plus 4 hours of work and one gallon of gas and he has a great piece of survival equipment.

When storing gasoline for vehicles or a generator remember to use the fuel within 4 to 6 months. If the fuel is going to be sitting for a long period of time buy some stabilizer to put in the fuel so it will not go bad. If the fuel goes bad and you try to use it you could experience some major problems with your equipment.

I suggest getting at least a five gallon can and fill it up. Place a date on your calendar three months away. If you have not used the fuel by the date then put it in your vehicle so that the fuel never goes to waste. Then refill the gas can and renew the date on the calendar. This way you will always have useable gasoline without fear of break downs or harming the equipment.

There is a way to make your own gas and with this gas you can run an engine or a generator. This idea has been around since the 1800's but has gone by the wayside. It is called Wood Gas. A wood gasifier is actually a very simple thing to make and harness. The simplest way involves two metal containers and a pipe.

What I have done in the past was to cut a metal 55 gallon drums barrel top off. Then find another metal container that is enclosed with a small opening in the top. Place the enclosed container inside the 55 gallon drum and place wood all around the inside container. Break up more wood into small chunks or chips and fill up the enclosed container though the small opening.

Now put a pipe on the inner container and secure it so that anything going in or out of the container has to pass through the pipe and try to ensure there are no gaps to prevent leakage. Now light a fire in the 55 gallon drum and make sure the fire engulfs the inside container. Once the inner container reaches about 451 degrees, the wood chips inside the enclosed container begin to break down into charcoal and give off methane gas.

Steam should start rising out of the top of the pipe. Once the container reaches 451 degrees then you can put a flame to the top of the pipe and the gas coming out of the pipe will ignite. If you have a gas operated generator then you can run a hose from the top of the pipe to the carburetor of the generator. This will now run the generator all off of just burning wood. This is a crude method but it will work. You do have to be careful with the tar and sludge that can come off of the wood if you're using scrap wood. There are Gasifier kits that can get you completely off the grid for less than ten thousand dollars. I am still experimenting and researching this topic and I invite you to do the same.

Back in World War II in Europe fuel was used for the military only and could not be purchased or even found by most citizens. Farmers began adding the wood gas stoves to their vehicles and tractors. This proved to be an effective and efficient way to get around or plow a field. Most people I talk to about a wood gasifier have no idea what it is and didn't even know it exists.

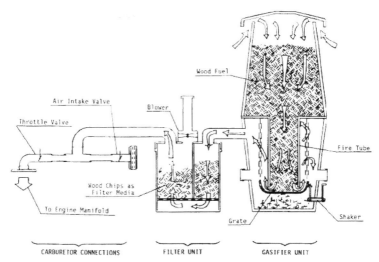

Fig. 1-3. Schematic view of the stratified, downdraft gasifier.

The schematic above is provided by
www.FEMA.org. FEMA's website is geared to being
prepared and helping the public. However FEMA
can't help everyone in a large scale disaster. You
need to stand up and help yourself.

Most people have a BBQ in the back yard these days.
The BBQ's will be most people's salvation until the
propane starts to run out. Some people only have the
small camp stoves that use the smaller bottles of
propane. If things get bad people are going to be
climbing into backyards to steal propane bottles. If
you have a BBQ that you can move you may want to
bring it inside until you want to use it. If you have a
BBQ island I recommend that you bring the propane
tank inside until you need it. If you don't a midnight
marauder just might find a prize in your backyard.

If you only have a camp stove that uses the small propane bottles then I suggest that you still buy a large propane tank and a refill valve. With the refill valve you can refill the small bottles making it easier to store propane than storing 50 small bottles. It is also cost effective to buy in bulk versus the small bottles.

When the power goes out it is a good idea to be stocked up on candles, Kerosene lamps or wicks to use with olive oil. I suggest that if you have candles to leave them in the freezer until you want to use them. By doing this you will increase the burn time of the candle and they drip less. I prefer to use a Tallow candle they burn brighter than other candles.

Another good item to have around is a crank powered lantern. With just one minute of cranking you get thirty minutes or more of light. These lanterns come in all shapes and sizes and are relatively cheap.

If the power goes out and you need a candle or a small flame to warm a can of soup then here is what you need.

A metal container such as a tuna can.
One piece of cloth.
One paper clip.
One table spoon of olive oil.

First open a can of tuna and eat the contents and clean out the can.

Next bend the paper clips outer end straight up and twist the cloth around the point of the paper clip. Then pull the ends of the cloth through the inner portion of the paper clip to keep it in place.

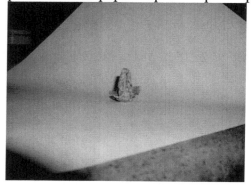

Then pour in the olive oil.

Soak the wick in the oil and place the wick into the middle of the can. Light the wick and enjoy your candle. Note: the can will get hot, place it on a hot pad or a trivet. If you place a wire rack over the flame it will heat or cook small portions in a pinch. With one tablespoon of olive oil the candle burned for about one hour.

If you don't think you have a rack to use over a candle or heat source then consider this, pull the wire rack out of your stove and put it on a couple bowls. This gives clearance for you to place a candle or heat source under the rack enabling you to cook or heat.

If you are a handy person then there is another type of stove that you can make called a rocket stove. The rocket stove can be made out of multiple cans of various sizes. I used one paint can, a spaghetti sauce can and a soup can.

First I cut a hole into the side of the paint can at the bottom the same size as the small soup can. I then did the same on the medium spaghetti sauce can.

I then check the fit of the cans and prepared to place them all together.

Check the fit of the cans and make sure the sauce can is centered in the paint can.

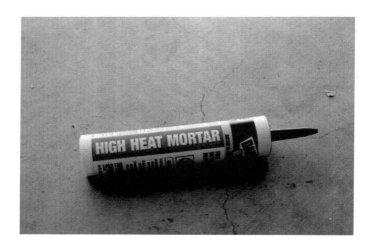

I then used some high temp fireplace mortar to seal the cans together. Make sure to seal all the gaps and don't be afraid to use a lot of mortar to seal everything up.

Next use a can opener and cut off the top lip of the paint can. Then using a piece of scrape tin cut out a ring that will slide into the paint can and around the sauce can.

Now cover the sauce can with a rag and secure the rag with a rubber band and pour Vermiculite in the void between the sauce can and the paint can. You can also use sand for the insulation however it makes the rocket stove heavy. The Vermiculite performs the same function with very little added weight.

Now install the tin ring and seal it to both cans using the high temp mortar.

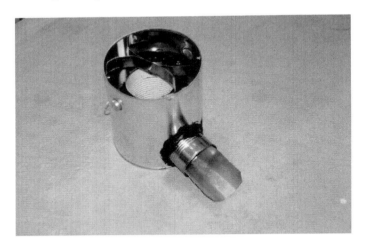

Lastly add a few scrap pieces of tin to the top for a place to hold a pot or pan. Then cut a small piece of tin and bend it slightly to fit in the soup can to act as a tray to hold longer sticks.

The Rocket Stove is a very efficient type of stove with a design that incorporates a venturi effect that will help burn hotter and longer.

If you ever decide to put decorative lights around your home buy the solar powered ones. This way if you lose power you can simply walk outside and grab a couple of your lights and use them throughout the night. The next morning put the lights back so that they have a chance to recharge so you can use them again.

When it comes to life without power one would have to think about what would happen if America was to be hit with an EMP (electromagnetic pulse). There are two countries (Iran and North Korea) that hate us and have been developing nuclear and electromagnetic bombs. Any nuclear weapon or an E-bomb that is detonated in the atmosphere about 250 miles above the ground would affect the entire

United States with an EMP sending us back one hundred years in an instant.

To protect electronic equipment the items need to be placed into a Faraday box. A Faraday box is a metal box that is grounded so that electronic waves pass through the box and into the ground keeping the items inside the metal box safe. There are limited tests for electromagnetic pulse and some experts say that even items kept in a metal filing cabinet could be saved from an EMP. If you decide to incorporate a Faraday box into your preps then I would suggest placing items like batteries, LED flashlights, solar cells, an inverter and a couple radios into the box.

Be sure to line the inside of the metal box with rubber lining to protect your items. If items are left touching the metal the EMP could still pass through item damaging the item. If you have an understanding about electronics then you could place an ohm meter, soldering iron and solder along with a large variety of diodes and resisters in the Faraday box to repair your electronics after an EMP.

We live in a petroleum based economy. If the oil goes away or the price goes so high that the normal person cannot afford to put gas in their vehicle to get to work, society will begin to fold. Truck drivers will stop hauling or go on strike. If there is a break down in the transportation of goods, stores will not get restocked and the shelves will go bare then the problems start. Soon the utilities begin to shut down and we are on our own.

8) Skills and the Barter System

When it comes to surviving an event you have to use what you have. If what you have is skills then use them. For someone who has automotive skills may be very valuable to someone trying to get out of town but broke down. The auto mechanic can use his skills to gain gear, food or needed supplies. When money is no longer worth the paper it is printed on then the barter system comes into full effect. The more you have to barter with the better you will weather the storm. Food, water, ammo, and fuel will all be at a premium and worth more than most people will have, leaving them at a severe disadvantage.

When preparing you should take a moment and think about what you have to offer to others in order to gain something that you don't have that could better your situation. Just remember if you are in a meltdown of society then you have to be careful with who you barter with. Try to stay away from strangers. People who live by you or know you are less likely to rob or injure you. However if a neighbor is desperate they can become dangerous.

As humans we like to think that we are above the animal kingdom. But deep down we all have a self preservation mechanism that kicks in and we can become an animal ourselves. When bartering, keep this in mind. You need food, water and shelter to survive. So it would not be wise to trade any of these things away. If you don't believe that you have any skills to trade then you may want to find a hobby or skill that you can learn. It never hurt anyone to learn something new.

There are a few things that you can collect to help you in your bartering needs. Whether you drink or not, it is not a bad idea to buy liquor when it is on sell and store it. Liquor will last extremely long and can be use by alcoholics or for medical purposes. Ammo would be a huge barter tool however it is probably wise to keep all of your ammo. It would be a good idea to also start saving all of your shell casings when you go shooting. It is also advisable to pick up as many shell casings that are in good condition as possible after shooting because they are a great bartering item for people who reload ammunition.

In hard times people who reload will trade or pay top dollar to obtain the precious brass. After shooting at the range I pick up all brass available regardless of calibers lying around as well as shotgun shells. I then separate the brass and place it in bags to be used or traded among other reloaders.

Batteries or candles would also be good for barter as long as you have extra. Now when bartering you need to find someone that has what you need and needs what you have extra. Toilet paper may be a really good barter product, everyone needs it. You can never have too much toilet paper; it never goes bad and has multiple uses.

If you have your survival garden going then you may have more produce than you can consume. The extra produce can be a great bartering tool, again be careful who you barter with. If you barter with a desperate neighbor they may visit your garden under the cover of night and steal more of your food. If you grow a garden it may be a good idea to learn how to can your own produce.

By canning your own food you can keep things from going bad and have a life skill that the younger generations have forsaken. Most of our grandparents canned food out of necessity during the growing seasons to help them get through the harsh winters. Why should we be so different? I believe we should learn to can now for the hard times ahead. Just for a moment let's say nothing happens. You can still use the food that you grew and you know it has no pesticides or chemicals to harm you or your family. Life skills can only help you. They will not take anything any from you.

When it comes to skills, making fire seems very basic but there are many tips and tricks to help you make a fire in all kinds of weather. Fire is a necessity because it cooks your food, keeps you warm and helps you with a multitude of various tasks. When building a fire in damp or wet conditions matches may not work. There are magnesium fire starters and other types of fire starters that can be very handy.

One different method of making a fire is to connect fine-grade steel wool to the positive and negative terminals of a 9-volt battery to create a glowing fire starter. Another thing you can do is go to the store and buy some Magic Candles. These are the trick candles that cannot be blown out once lit. It's a fun birthday party trick but it makes a get way to start a fire on a windy day when a normal match just won't work.

One of the methods that I use is to buy a package of cotton balls and turn them into fire tender. Take out the cotton balls and stretch, fluff and spread out the cotton ball. Then add a little bit of Vaseline. Once you have a small amount of Vaseline on the cotton ball you roll it up and squeeze out and get rid of all the excess Vaseline. This makes the cotton balls extremely flammable. I then store them in a small film container until I'm ready to use them. Once I am ready to build a fire I remove one of the Vaseline cotton balls fluff and spread the cotton ball out. It only takes a spark to ignite the cotton and once ignited it will burn for up to three minutes.

Another way to make a fire easily can be made using a Magnesium fire starter.

The magnesium starter is easy to use. First use the blade provided with the starter or a knife and scrape off some of the magnesium onto some tender or paper. Now use the blade or knife edge on the flint and it will ignite the magnesium which can burn as hot as 5000 degrees.

There are a hundred different ways to make a fire and I invite you to find several ways that work for you. If you only depend on one way and that way is not working in the conditions you are currently in then you are left with nothing. I try to live by the old saying, "two is one and one is none" because if your one doesn't work you have none.

Farming skills can come in very handy. Check with your city codes. Here in the southwest most cities allow a few chickens per parcel of land. If you decide to raise a few chickens make sure that you get all hens. They are quite; it is the roosters that crows in the morning make your neighbors hate you. Chickens can be fun to raise. They will eat all of your weeds in the yard and if you use their poop in a compost bin it becomes some of the best fertilizer you can make for your survival garden. Chickens will also eat every bug around your house. The only down fall is that chickens poop a lot and everywhere.

If you want to get a few chickens you will need to build them a coup. The chickens can be kept in the coup at all times or let out for a few hours a day to scrounge for food to reduce grain feeding them. Chickens will also eat just about anything. If you have a few leftovers throw them in the coup and the chickens will devoir it.

Most chickens will lay between 100-300 eggs a year. If you are in tough times and have to work hard to get through the day you need protein. Eggs are protein packed and can help keep you strong in hard times. Also if times get too tough or the chickens stop laying eggs, then they become dinner.

If it comes down to it you can also keep the chickens in a cage indoors to prevent thieves from taking your eggs or your chicken for their food needs. The cage would have to be cleaned often and this is a worst case scenario. If you are in the suburbs and have an acre of land or more then you may want to think about getting some other animals that can benefit you during times of need. Goats are a good animal to have around.

Goats can provide you with milk which can be turned into butter. The milk or butter can be consumed or bartered for other goods. Also goats are nature's lawnmowers. If you have a large grassy area you will not need to mow anymore the goats will keep the grass very short. Goats will eat any portion of leftover fruits and vegetables that would normally be discarded. Also in desperate times goat meat will provide much needed protein.

Skills are going to be the difference between survivors and victims'. I recommend that you start looking on the internet and print out "how to" articles and place them into a binder as a Just-In-Case book. A Just-In-Case book can be worth its weight in gold if it comes to a time when there is no power and no internet to found out how to do simple things that people just don't know how to do anymore.

If you find yourself in the middle of an event and you have to live with only what you have then you need to know what to barter away and what not to. With no stores open and no power or running water people will be trying to find ways to get what they need. This is going to be true for you as well. No matter how much you think you are prepared there is always something that you are going to wish you had or had more of. There are certain items that you should be stocked up on to be used as bartering items.

By using coupons to shop you can get most toiletries for free or extremely cheap by combining them with the stores sales. In bad times things like razors, soap, toilet paper, deodorant, wet wipes, hand sanitizer and shampoo are going to be in short supply. These can be good bartering items if it will not take away from your essential supply.

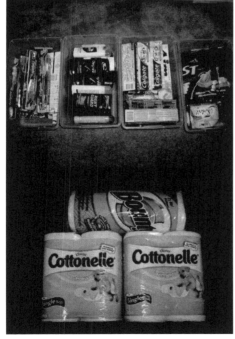

There are a few food items that you may keep extras around to barter with. These include salt, sugar, peanut butter, baking powder, yeast, and cereal. These items can be purchased cheap and last for a long time giving you more bartering power.

If you know how to can your own food then you are leaps and bounds above the rest. People who know how to can will be able to preserve more food and store it for a long period of time. If you need to barter food, canned food can be a worth a lot to people who are in need. When you think about it canned foods don't cost you much money just your time. If you want to learn more about canning check out farmgal.tripod.com.

One thing that you may try to get is several Fresnel lens or parabolic mirrors. If someone wants to barter with you, you may be able to get just about anything you want if you show the prospective barterer how powerful the Fresnel lens or parabolic mirror can be and how to use it. If drinking water is in short supply then you may be able to profit from others greatly by using your skills of water procurement or distilling pool water. Having water to drink is the most important thing out there next to air to breath and followed by food to eat.

When it comes to the barter system some things can become extremely valuable such as drinking water or the ability to make it drinkable. By stocking up on a few bags of pool shock you have the ability to make up to12000 gallons of water drinkable. 1/8 oz of powder will make one gallon of bleach. In a survival situation bleach and potable water could give you a huge advantage in the barter system.

If it ever comes down to a collapse of the dollar or hyperinflation then the barter system will be in full effect. However Gold and Silver should still hold its value and will return as a currency and can be used for trade. It would be a good idea to obtain gold and silver coins and keep them in a safe place in your home. If you leave your home to bug out be sure and take your coins with you.

For those of you who are in fear of the collapsing dollar or want to have gold, silver or a precious metal as a long term investment or even a backup to your paper money. I suggest too start by looking through your change. When looking through your change be sure to save any pennies that are from the years 1909 to 1981. These pennies are 95% copper and are actually worth 2.12 cents at current prices. The markets will show us that as the dollar is devalued precious metals go up. Pennies made from 1982 on are 97.5% zinc which is only worth .006 cents.

I usually drop my change into a jar every day when I come home and on average out of about 50 pennies I find about 10 that are 1981 or older. Then when it comes to silver if you have any quarters or dimes minted before 1965 they are worth their weight in silver. A quarter minted between 1932 and 1964 at current prices is worth $3.44 due to its silver content. Quarters that have been minted from 1965 to 2009 only contain .44 cents of silver if melted down.

Since I have discovered this information I have begun checking my loose change and it amazes me that there is still so many coins out there in circulation that have been minted before 1965. If you can buy pure silver or gold then that is better than loose change. It is wise to print out the information of coin worth and coin prices to be placed into your Just-In-Case book you can now argue any points for bartering purposes. One of the best websites that I have come across for coin worth and price is Coinflation.com.

The barter system will save your life and if you are prepared you will be on the top of the food chain.

9) The dirty truth about sanitation.

If society begins to tank and you are trying to ride out the event inside your home there are several things that you can do to keep the sanitation going.

First, start living by the rule "If it's yellow let it mellow and if it's brown flush it down". As long as the water is flowing, your toilet system will still operate. Now the sewer system may only last a week or two. However your sewer system is set up on gravity feed system which means as long as you have water you can still flush the toilet.

If you have an abundance of water such as a pool in the back yard or a rain barrel then all you have to do is use about one gallon of water and place it into the back of the toilet reservoir. Then you can flush down the brown and not have to worry about foul smells or getting you or your family sick from bacteria. When you wash dishes or clean yourself don't just throw the water away. Put the water in the toilet tank to help flush away your waste.

If the water and sewer system is down for an extended period of time there could be a problem developing. As people try to use the downed system with no pumps working, the sanitation stations shut down and the sewer could become backed up. If the water has been off for a week or so it is advisable to shut off the main water valve to the house to help prevent sewer back flow into the house. Then find the main sewer pipe which should be in the front yard and locate the cleanout port. Open the port and place a plug in the pipe to block any backflow and replace the cap. Once your crisis is over, open the plumbing and remove the plug to resume normal operation.

If the sewer system backs up into the house during times with no power or running water your home will become unlivable and you will have to relocate. If you have nowhere else to go this could be detrimental to your already bad situation. It is also advisable to turn off the valves to the toilets. If you used the bath tub to store water in, the weight of the water bags should help block the drain to prevent backflow.

Now if you can no longer flush you waste down for any reason then get all of the water out of the toilet and place a trash bag in the bowl just like you would place a garbage bag into a trash can. Then place the lid of the toilet down and you can now do your stuff. Once you get done remove the bag and get as much air out of the bag as possible. Next tie a knot in the top of the bag to prevent smells or spillage.

You have two chooses. You can dig a big hole in your back yard and begin disposing of waste there or place all of the waste in a container like a garbage can to be disposed of at a later date. This part is up to you and your situation; just remember it needs to be contained and away from your water supply to keep you safe. If you are on a well do not bury your waste in the ground where it could seep down to your water supply and make you sick.

If you are in an area where you can build fires and no one will come and bother you then it might be a good idea to burn your waste. By burning the waste all of the bacteria will be consumed and you will only left with ashes that can be used for other things. One thing to consider is to try and get a supply of hand sanitizer around to keep the germs down and keep you healthy.

When it comes to it, you need to keep yourself free of any waste to stay healthy. This is best accomplished by using a spray bottle filled with water and a little bit of dish soap. Once you're done simply spray yourself with the solution and let it wash away any fecal matter and then if you have toilet paper available wipe off any remaining water.

When throwing out your trash it is a good idea to separate your trash by removing perishables from the non-perishables. You can greatly reduce the amount of stinky and bacteria generating trash by removing the packaging. You can use three trash bags, one for cardboard then another for metal cans and the finial one for plastics. These bags can be placed on the side of the house to be used if needed for special projects or just stored. Now your garbage can may last weeks by throwing out bad food or waste only.

When it comes to sanitation there are certain things you can keep around that no matter how long you keep it, it won't go bad. Toilet paper will forever be in demand and it will not spoil or diminish in quality over time. I recommend that you stock as much as you can. Baby wipes and soaps are items that you can use forever as well. With these two items a little care is to be taken to keep them usable for long periods of time. Soap needs to be kept in a steady climate until use and the baby wipes should be kept in something like a zip lock bag to keep them moist and fresh.

Garbage bags are another thing to have on hand. They keep your trash and waste contained and sealed to help keep you and your family healthy. You will always use garbage bags. I suggest buying in bulk that way you get them cheaper and always have a sufficient supply. This can be done by finding them on sale or at your local wholesaler to get the best bargain. But it is important to stay stocked up. For just one moment think about trying to go through life without toilet paper, soap, and trash bags. What would you do? These items are not a necessity for life but they do they make it easier.

When it comes to history we have to learn from it or we are destined to repeat it. In WWII the British were able to defeat the Germans in North Africa due to personal hygiene. All of the German soldiers were suffering from dysentery ultimately crushing their moral, and their will to fight causing their defeat.

10) Hunting and food gathering.

When there is no food in the stores and you have to start fending for yourself you need to have options. If you live in an urban environment then I would suggest buying a BB gun. With a BB gun you can hunt birds and small animals like rabbits and squirrels. If you are hunting rabbits or other small game you need to use pellets on them and use BB's for birds. Starting at $100.00 you can buy a break barrel pellet gun and with the use of a scope and PBA pellets you can achieve 1200 FPS with great accuracy. This can be a valuable asset when going after medium sized game.

A BB or pellet gun can be very quiet and keep you feed without alerting your neighbors. As you prepare your survival gear it is a good idea to include a bag of bird seed. Once you throw out the bird seed it only takes a few hours and you will have birds flying in to feast on the seed.

When hunting small game and using a pump style air rifle, make sure to use the maximum pumps to deliver a lethal shot. When shooting any game with any weapon try to take a shot hitting the game in the chest area. If the game is on all four legs, aim for the side just behind the front leg. Both of these shots should hit major organs and cause the game to die quickly.

When going after some bigger game you well want to have a high power rifle such as a 30-06 or a 270 Winchester. I like these two calibers because after reloading for some years I like being able to load a 90 grain 270 bullet for small game and varmint hunting or a 180 grain 270 bullet for hunting deer and Elk. This is what I use, if you have something that works for you that's fine as long as you have something.

With the taking of any game then comes the gutting and skinning of the animal. Removing the pellet or feathers is going to have small differences for each animal. I could go on all day long on how to skin and gut an animal but if you need to know how to field dress an animal then I suggest that you get your hunting license and go hunting with a friend who knows what to do and learn how first hand.

If you live by a lake or river then fishing could be your best resource for food. Even if you don't fish now you can go to your local Wal-Mart and purchase a cheap rod and reel for around $20. Along with the rod and reel get some hooks and other accessories and store them. If all hell breaks loose then you can dig for your own worms or use bugs, lizards, or food like corn and start landing fish to help boost your food supply.

Something to remember is that most of the bugs, worms and lizards that you can use for bait can also be eaten as food. They all have a nutritional value and are full of protein giving you energy in any bad situation. Now this may be your last resort and most people today wouldn't eat a worm if their life depended on but one day it just might.

Now when it comes to edible plants most people will not eat roots or plants even when they are starving because they just don't have the knowledge of what is ok to eat and what is poisonous for you. There are books out there that are dedicated to this topic and I highly recommend that you purchase one of these books or make your own. When you go camping it is always fun to pull the book out and show your children that you can survive on by eating only what Mother Nature has given us.

Just remember if you have never eaten only wild plants then you should start slow. Only eating wild plants can give you a stomach ache and make you think that you may have made a mistake and picked a poisonous plant when it is simply that your system is not used to it. I have seen people try to make whole meals for an entire day out of roots, plants, nuts and berries. Soon they were not feeling good. If you start by snacking between meals and work your way into it you will be just fine.

When you are out gathering food there are other things that you can be mindful of and keep a lookout for these things. If you are in need of some glue to fasten something together then you can cut the bark off of a pine tree and get to the sap. Once you get to the sap you can apply the sap to anything to glue it and make it water proof. I have used a flat piece of leather, folded up the sides and used sap to glue it. By doing this I made a bowl that I could eat out of or gather water or use for just about anything.

When eating wild plants, most plants can be eaten however you need to know what part of the plant to eat. For example you can make a drink from Elderberry flowers and fruit but you should stay away from the rest of the plant as it is poisonous. Wild plants can be one of the most abundant sources of food you can find in hard times. Beware of berries, only a hand full of the berries you find will actually be edible.

If it comes down to it a person can eat grass. You can also use the inner portion of a pine tree and make a flour substitute. Most leaves are edible and can provide much needed nutrition. If you live by the ocean then you should look for seaweed. Seaweed is high in nutrition and vitamin C. I don't like the taste of it but it will help you survive. Seaweed can be found in some bodies of fresh water as well but not all. This is just a few examples of natures buffet.

When looking for a book on wilderness survival and edible plants look for one that has color pictures if possible. By seeing color pictures verses drawings is a huge advantage. I had a book that had only drawings of plants and it did not help me very much. In the previous chapters I wrote about making a Just-In-Case book. What I suggest is to go on the internet and download pictures of edible plants and print them out. Now place the pictures in your Just-In-Case book.

Looking up pictures and searching the internet can take a long time and I used up one color printer cartridge which cost me about $7 more than a book would have. However I now have a custom book with color photos of each edible plant and each poisonous plant so I know what to stay away from. This book has served me well on many camping trips.

Just remember never eat anything that you have not identified and know 100% what parts to eat and that it is safe.

11) The final countdown

When it comes to the American way of life, we all know that it is going to change one day. It may be tomorrow or one hundred years from now. There may be a terrorist attack on the United States so server that it devastates the way we live and thrive. Then there is Mother Nature, she can be one of the most destructive forces on the planet and we are at her mercy. Man is the second most destructive force on the planet. These are some of the reasons we need to prepare. This book is simply written to help people like myself to prepare for the future. By preparing you have placed yourself and your family just a little higher up on the food chain.

If the Swine flu or the bird flu hits America hard would you be able to quarantine yourself in your home and have everything you need to survive for two weeks or one month? If civil unrest broke out in your town could you hunker down or bug out with everything that you need to survive? Will you be ready to defend your family and your supplies from intruders?

As I am writing this book I see on the news people yelling and screaming about the Health Care bill and the Cap and Trade bill. Like I said before if you want to see the future look to the past. Germany pasted a Cap and Trade bill several years ago and now they are fighting inflationary prices. Canada has socialized Heath Care and their citizens come to America to get medical care. Our leaders are driving our country into the ground. If you are having trouble getting motivated to get prepared just watch the news.

I hope that after you finish reading this you want to learn more about preparing and survival. I am a self taught man and it has taken me years to get to the point I am at today. I hope that I have jump started you and helped you get ahead of the game. In today's society things change so fast that you have to be able to adapt. If you ask anyone if they think of bad scenarios and then think of a way to conquer the situation they would most likely say no.

If you think about it, this is why the Military and Law Enforcement train for unseen situations. When they train they come up with new techniques to counter the situation so they can be victorious every time. To be a survivor you need to start training. Even if the training you do is only mental, it is training. If you practice a technique and it comes time to use it you don't waste time having to think about the action needed, you just act.

With any situation you need to have a plan. In your plan you need to take into account if you are going to weather the storm alone or if you are going to stay with family. If you have fortified your home and have a vast amount of supplies at your home then evaluate if family will come stay with you. Now with more people your food supplies will deplete faster however security could be better. You should talk to the family or friends that would possibly come and stay with you and make a deal.

If you are going to open your home to others they should bring something to the table. If you have elderly parents or young kids try to think of things they may need that differs from you. Talk to your family or friends and make a list of things that they have that in an event they should bring to your home or things you need to take to theirs. With family and friends at your home or you at theirs, the one thing both of you need to have is patience. Stress and close quarters equals tension.

Be careful if times get bad and it is down to people dying, everyone gets greedy and self preservation occurs, this includes even friends and sometimes family. This is worst case scenario.

If we enter a full collapse you are on your own. Law enforcement may no longer be there to help everyone and what you have is it. At this point you have to decide what you are going to do. Do you have everything you need or are you going to venture outside in search of more supplies? If you do go out try to not standout. Stay hidden and do not draw attention to yourself.

If you need supplies and decide to venture out for things like fuel, then try and find abandoned cars with a plastic gas tanks and drill a hole on the bottom of the tank and let it drain out. This is a lot faster than trying to siphon out the fuel and by drilling you can get all of the fuel out. Look inside the vehicles, you may find things like reflective sunshades to make a solar oven or first aid kits, flash lights, tools and other valuable things. Also if you are able to take the vehicles battery, this will provide you with more options for power. If you are able to get a good vehicle battery you should also remove the lights and wiring, that way you can use them with the battery to light up your home.

Make sure that you take at least one weapon with you to defend yourself as well. If you do not have any weapons or you are the type of person who believes you could not hurt someone then at least carry pepper spray or a can of wasp spray. Wasp spray can spray attackers from up to 20 feet away with the same results as pepper spray. Next look around now at commercial buildings and temporary stop lights for solar panels. These may be something that you can use if all hell breaks loose.

When scavenging, don't just look for the things you need. If you see a flashlight but believe you have plenty and do not need it. Remember, barter could become the way of life. Others will give you something very valuable for the flashlight you were about to leave behind.

If you venture out it may be beneficial to obtain a shopping cart. If fuel is no longer available and you are without any type of vehicle a shopping cart can be a great resource for being able to move large or heavy objects or multiple items to other locations with relative ease. Children cannot walk long distances like adults so a shopping cart may become the stroller of the post apocalyptic world.

Also it may be a good idea to have a few mouse traps on hand to set and try to catch a snack if it comes down to a survival situation.

If you have neighbors that went to stay with other family and they have a pool or you have a community pool in the neighborhood then you could get water from these sources.

A pool like the one in the picture can hold 10,000 to 15,000 gallons of water. As long as you prepare the water it should be sufficient to get you through any event.

It comes down to the fact that you will need food, water, shelter, defense, and knowledge of how survive without power or running water.

In the Army I learned a phrase the 7 P's "Proper prior planning prevents piss poor performance" Hopefully my proper prior planning has become yours and will prevent any piss poor performance.

12) Research

Here are some topics that you may be interested in and should research more. A full book could be written on each one of these topics and some have been. Arm yourself with knowledge and you will become a true soldier in the fight for survival.

1) Gasification
2) Fresnel Lens and parabolic mirrors
3) Solar energy
4) Solar oven
5) Water purification
6) Food and water storage
7) Canning and Mylar packaging
8) Reloading ammunition
9) Camping and wilderness survival
10) Edible plants

There is so much information out there on tips and tricks that will help you out in a time of crises. I invite you to now take on the task of survival for yourself. I hope that I have sparked an interest and that my ideas and tips help you. I believe I have shown you only a seed. Now as technology advances and you find out new tricks or tips and even old ones that resurface there is a whole tree of knowledge out there.

Now that you have finished this book I want you to try something. One weekend go camping and while out in the woods think of everything you may need if you were going to stay out there for a week or two and even up to a month. On another weekend turn off the power and water to your house, then within the two days time you well find out what you need to have around to prepare yourself for any disaster, be it manmade or from Mother Nature.

When an emergency is upon you the time for preparation has passed.

The prudent see danger and take refuge, but the simple keep going and suffer for it. Proverbs 27:12

It may not survival of the fittest anymore, its maybe survival of the smartest.

Prepare and prepare, oh yeah and prepare.

13) Resources and Sources:

For questions and further survival or preparedness information please visit survivalandpreparedness.com. This forum has the most experienced survivalist on the web. Become a member and get your survival or preparedness questions answered.

www.seattleoil.com/Flyers/Earthbox.pdf

www.Earthboxresearch.com

www.greenpowerscience.com

www.boxotruth.com

www.fbi.gov

www.solarcooking.org

www.fema.org

www.ldscatalog.org

www.asce.org

www.preparingwisely.com

If you have any questions or for further information you can contact me at urbansurvivalist@gmail.com

Use this check list to inventory what you have or
what you need.

Checklist

1)
_____
2)
_____
3)
_____
4)
_____
5)
_____
6)
_____
7)
_____
8)
_____
9)
_____
10)
_____
11)
_____
12)
_____
13)
_____
14)
_____

15)

16)

17)

18)

19)

20)

21)

22)

23)

24)

25)

26)

27)

28)

29)

30)

31)

32)
_____
33)
_____
34)
_____
35)
_____
36)
_____
37)
_____
38)
_____
39)
_____
40)
_____
41)
_____
42)
_____
43)
_____
44)
_____
45)
_____
46)
_____
47)
_____
48)
_____

49)

50)

I have added several pages for your notes, this way you can add your own tips and tricks to this book and take it with you. Now this can be your personnel Just In Case book.

Notes

_____

_____

_____

_____

_____

_____

_____

_____

_____

_____

_____

_____

_____

_____

_____

_____

_____

_____

_____

_____

_____

_____

_____

_____

_____

_____

_____

_____

_____

_____

_____

The End

Printed in Great Britain
by Amazon.co.uk, Ltd.,
Marston Gate.